HIGH CLASS NATIVES
Ballroom Dancers
&
Mbira Players

by

Alf E.F. Muronda

REPRINTED - February - 2026

ISBN 978-1-965398-29-6
© Elfigio F Muronda
Publisher: MASAKA PUBLISHING MEDIA HOUSE
alf@cp7sisters.com

Table of Contents

ACTS of THE PLAY

Dedication

For my grandfathers, vana Mupamombe nana Unedhoro

For my brothers Richard L Muronda and Dennis Nyagwaya and my uncle Biggie Chirikumarara, our family heroes of the struggle for Zimbabwe.

For the late Chiwoniso Maraire, my friend, one of Zimbabwe's greatest mbira virtuosos. In our friendship her spirit is reflected in this work.

Acknowledgements

Telling the story which became this play started a long time ago. However, the play would never have seen the light of day were it not for the late great Beverly Robinson, Theater Arts Professor, who became an inspiration and a muse in my life when I was at the University of California in Los Angeles. No words can ever express the depth of my gratitude to her.

Thank you to my family, especially my wife, Val for giving me space and time to write and a special thanks to my friend, fellow writer, Jaky Tafara Chimutashu, whose relentless banter, wit and criticism helped me survive and overcome my doubts about letting my antagonistic characters be who they are without acting as their public relations agent.

If this work is worth your time to read this book or to watch the play performed on stage, all credit goes to the people mentioned above, if not, it's all on me.

HIGH CLASS NATIVES
Ballroom Dancers & Mbira Players

THEMATIC DESCRIPTION

Against a backdrop of racial oppression, African political aspirations, and the war against the white minority rule of the country, the play is a tragedy set in the late 1970s in Beatrice Cottages, a residential section of one of the African townships in the outskirts of Salisbury in Rhodesia. The musical play, *HIGH CLASS NATIVES,* uses the metaphors of European classical ballroom dance music, and Zimbabwe's traditional African mbira music, as a commentary on the clash of cultures in one family forced by the circumstance of the war to live under one roof.

CHARACTERS

Majasi: an old African man (Sekuru)

Rwizi: Majasi's older son (40ish)

Sally: Rwizi's wife (late 30s)

Belinda: Sally's friend (Auntie Bee)

Sam: Belinda's husband

John: Rwizi and Sally's 6-year-old son

Tino: John's friend same age (6yrs)

Andrew: Rwizi's 19-year-old brother

Arimando   Houseboy (servant)

Chaitezvi: Majasi's age mate and friend

Night Visitor: Old woman, Sally's aunt

Mbira Players: Chamu, Muchazo (Andrew's girlfriend) Max, Ticha, Tawanda & Zodwa

Mr. Mlambo: Neighbourhood house homeowner

Political Activists: 7 African men and 2 women.

Comrades: 2 Freedom Fighters (guerrillas)

MC: James Goto, An African man

McIntyre: A white man

Photographer: Young man

Guests: Formally attired couples: white, Indian, Coloured (mixed race) & Africans.

SYNOPSIS

The play is a slice of life in Rhodesia circa 1977. The play in nine acts, transpires over a four-month period. The story centers around the life of the Chotos, who live in the Beatrice Cottages enclave which, at that time, was a few rungs above the rest of the government designated African people's housing in the sprawling National African Township, now known as Mbare Township, located on the outskirts of Salisbury (now known as Harare) the capital city of the country.

The recently widowed Choto family patriarch, Majasi, finds himself living in Beatrice Cottages at the home of his oldest son, Rwizi. His village home was burnt to the ground by the Rhodesian Army forces in Mhondoro African Reservation after they had killed his old wife as punishment for her having obliged some guerrilla fighters who were passing through, who had brought some meat with them that they needed cooked for a meal.

Rwizi, who has done well for himself in the capital city of Salisbury at a time when management jobs and social positions were hard to come by for Africans in the minority white controlled country, is a deputy manager in the City of Salisbury's Revenue Services Department. His equally successful wife is Sally. She has a high-ranking position as Matron Nurse at Harare African General Hospital. Rwizi and Sally have a 6-year-old son, John. Sally's best friend is a fellow Nurse Matron, Belinda, who is married to Sam, a businessman. The two couples are considered upper middle class in the African community of that time.

When the story begins, Rwizi has come home from work accompanied by his 18-year-old younger brother, Andrew, who had arrived at his office late that afternoon from the boarding secondary school where he had just completed Form Four. Normally, Andrew would be going to their home located in the African reservation in Mhondoro where their village was, but there no longer was any home for Andrew in that

7

reservation in Mhondoro to go to. For that reason Andrew comes to town to visit his older brother who has been paying for his schooling to see about securing his future and his accommodations away from the dangerous war zones and the reservations.

That evening, in the ensuing private conversation between Rwizi and his wife in their bedroom, Sally makes it clear to her husband that she has no intention of accommodating his father nor his young brother in their house any longer than she must, and that she is only doing so to help him out with his relatives. She justifies her inhospitality on the premise that presence of these relatives of his in their home is going to be disruptive to her aim to raise their son, John, to be a European cultured person.

Rwizi owes his father a lot. It was his father who sold most of their family's small cattle herd to pay for his higher education which enabled him to land the management job in the Revenue Department of the City of Salisbury. It was also his father who loaned him the money for the down payment on the Beatrice Cottages house they live in, a fact he never shared with his wife Sally (justifying this omission to tell his wife about it behind the fact that it was a loan he paid back). Not only does Rwizi love his father and brother wholeheartedly but according to Shona native tradition, it also behooves him, as the oldest son in the family, to ensure the health and welfare of the whole family. Nonetheless, he has an equal obligation to his nuclear family and the society-page-life to which his wife aspires to.

Sally, an orphan and only child with no family relatives of her own, eschews most African traditions. She is determined to raise their son, John, to be a 'European' who only speaks the English language: an impractical task that is hard to accomplish under the best of circumstances but near impossible since her six-year-old boy, being a normal boy, likes to play with the other young boys in the neighborhood who happen not to have any use for the English language in their young lives.

Thus, Sally suddenly finds her carefully manicured nuclear family life being invaded by the pestilence of her husband's family from the African reservation villages who not only speak the tribal Shona vernacular language she abhors, but they also happen to be traditional African mbira music afficionados which is antithetical to everything she stands for.

Compounding an already untenable situation for Rwizi is another important aspect of their life being affected by what the war in the villages has wrought into their life. At the center of their social life is ballroom dancing to classical European music. The couple, who happen to be exceptionally talented ballroom dancers, are solid, passionate members of the Salisbury African Ballroom Dancing Club, a club affiliated with the larger Rhodesia Ballroom Dancing Association. So, besides the fact that Sally's aspirations for her son to grow up to be a European cultured man are now being jeopardized by the presence of Rwizi's Shona speaking father, it has become near impossible for them to practice their ballroom dancing steps in their living room. To Sally's annoyance, Rwizi's father spends most of his time listening to the government's radio station which broadcasts in native languages and plays mbira music specifically programmed for the country's African audience.

In that private conversation Rwizi and Sally had in their bedroom, Sally reminded Rwizi that the regional ballroom dancing competition, which she expects them to win, is four months away. Win or lose, she had already signed up their house to host the after-party to be attended by their white, Indian, African and Coloured ballroom dancing friends that night, at which the championship trophy will be presented. Sally stresses to Rwizi that she expects him to have made other living arrangements for his father whose traditional African-old -man presence in their house is not befitting of the European cultured nuclear family she wants to portray to her friends that night. When Rwizi demurs, Sally threatens to leave him with their son, if he does not comply with that demand before the ballroom dancing competition date.

Later that same evening, during dinner, Rwizi excuses himself from accompanying Sally to a scheduled ballroom dancing practice session because he is going to attend a political meeting in a house in the neighbourhood. Sally is aghast that her husband would forego going to a ballroom dancing practice session to spend time attending useless meetings with "uneducated Africans howling at the moon and clamouring for independence from their white benefactors". As much as it was irking him, Andrew restrains himself from countermanding Sally's condescending attitude to the aspirations of Africans who are protesting the country's white oppression. However, it reaches a point where he simply cannot take it any longer. Respectfully he lets Sally know his feelings about it all. Sally dismissively labels him a naive communist puppy. Rwizi prevails telling his wife that it is for their safety as a family that he must attend these meetings to keep up appearances as a supporter of the general African political angst with the white minority government. If he doesn't, he tells her, they will be labelled sell-outs and subject to violence from political thugs.

However unbeknown to Sally, who vehemently opposes the general African political movements seeking the removal of white rule in Rhodesia, her husband Rwizi is an ardent clandestine supporter of the liberation movements.

After dinner, Sally drives off to the ballroom dancing practice by herself, while Rwizi and his younger brother, Andrew, walk to the meeting at Mlambo's house. The meeting, held under the guise of a native Shona traditional ancestral mbira music *bira* (gathering) is attended by a mix of young and older men and women with men, including Rwizi, wearing animal fur hats on their heads and the women wearing wraparound coloured cloth around their waists, as a political statement. When Rwizi and Andrew arrive, the mbira players are already in session. To everyone's surprise and the mbira players' delight, Andrew, a mbira child prodigy turned virtuoso, picks up one of the mbiras laying on the floor and ends up leading the group in a succession of songs.

Sally's friend, Belinda, a frequent visitor at the Choto house, happens to respect and enjoy African customs and mbira music. She gets along famously with John and his Sekuru Majasi. She brings the two treats when she visits. On one of her visits, she surprises Majasi by presenting him with a brand-new hat for which the old man is visibly moved with gratitude.

Three months later we find the old man Majasi, who is sickly, still living at Rwizi and Sally's house. In the meantime, Rwizi has found accommodations for Andrew at Matapi Hostels, a squalid single men's hostel that sleeps 8 men to a room in bunkbeds. Andrew's daily search for a job is proving to be futile because the country of Rhodesia was then under UN economic sanctions, has a shrinking economy, making jobs scarce. Andrew walks five miles one way from Matapi Hostels, where he sleeps, to his brother's house in Beatrice Cottages where he eats his daily meal at lunch with his father. Considering his hopeless prospects of finding a job anytime soon, Andrew tells his father that other young people like himself were leaving the country to go to Mozambique and Zambia to train in guerrilla warfare and join the freedom fighters who were waging the war for the liberation of Rhodesia from white rule. Majasi tells Andrew that he understands his desire to avenge the death of his mother and the loss of their home. He asks Andrew to leave the vengeance for that which they have lost to their ancestors and tells him how much his presence makes his life worthwhile because, with his wife dead and gone, Andrew is the only one left to look after him. Andrew assures his father that he would not leave him.

In that scene, which transpires on the veranda looking out to the street, we learn that Andrew has developed a friendship with the mbira players he met when Rwizi took him to the political meeting in the neighbourhood the evening he arrived from boarding school. While sitting on the veranda visiting with his father, two of the band members Chamu and Muchazo stop by on their way to band practice at Mlambo's house. It turns out Muchazo, the girl who was singing and playing mbira that night, and Andrew have a romantic interest in each other. Chamu, who is the band leader, has been trying to recruit Andrew to join the group since that night when he had played with them. Andrew being busy looking for work has had sporadic visits with the group at practice when he could. Muchazo gives Andrew a surprise gift of a mbira which was bought for him with monies contributed to buy it from all the players in the group. Andrew decides to join the group.

In the next scene, there is no one on the stage except a cityscape painting that shows the City of Salisbury's Revenue Department Building. We hear a telephone conversation initiated by Sally to Rwizi while he is at work. She starts by excitedly telling Rwizi that their names were mentioned in the society page of the Rhodesia Herald newspaper as finalists in the regional ballroom dancing competition. Then she also announces to Rwizi that she knows that Rwizi has not been able to find a home for his father. Through her professional connections, she proudly tells him, she has found a suitable home for his father. She tells him that this particular old people's facility is a good place because it is administered by a former nursing school classmate of hers. Rwizi asks her where it is. She tells him it's in Plumtree. Rwizi protests that Plumtree is 300 miles away. Sally tells him that with the war going on in the country there are no vacancies in an any old people's homes in the country and that he should be grateful she has solved his problem for him. Rwizi is speechless.

A few days later, it is in the evening at Choto house. Both Majasi, who is not feeling well, and John have both gone to bed early. Rwizi and Sally have taken advantage of the absence of the two from the living room. They are dressed in their practice ballroom costumes for the rehearsal they are doing in preparation for the regional ballroom dancing competition. They are drinking cocktails and practicing their waltz and foxtrot dance steps with no care in the world when there is a knock at the door. Sally excuses herself to go to the bathroom while Rwizi attends to the door. When Sally returns, she sees that Rwizi has let an old woman with her bundle into their house. The old woman is sitting on the floor by the door. Sally turns around and calls Rwizi into their bedroom where she begins to chastise Rwizi for bringing in yet another relative of his into their home. Rwizi tells her the woman is not his relative, but hers.

Back in the living room Sally interrogates the woman who turns out to be Sally's mother's older sister whom she had never met. The old woman has come to Sally's home seeking refuge from the war like many other people from the villages. She tells them she got information about Sally's address from the mission school where Sally donates food and medicines regularly in Mutoko. Sally is so angry at this old woman's intrusion into her life after all these years; she goes into the kitchen to get a broom to beat the woman and throw her out of her house. Rwizi restrains Sally, giving the old woman the chance to escape Sally's seething anger.

It turns out that Sally is so upset because she is an only child who was born by a teenage woman who had been raped by her own father. Sally's mother, the pregnant teenager, the victim of the rape, was instead, banished by her family from her village home in Mutoko African reservation for that abomination. Cast out into the forest, the

13

teenage mother was rescued by a white missionary. She grew up as an orphan cared for by missionary charity schools in Mutoko.

That night, Sally reminds Rwizi that within the month there will be the ballroom dancing competition. She tells him that he has to move his father to Plumtree otherwise the bed space promised to her by her friend, the administrator of the facility, will be given to someone else.

A few days later, it is daytime at Mlambo house where the band practises. Andrew arrives tired from walking the five miles from Matapi Hostels to Beatrice Cottages. His tired face turns to elation when his girlfriend, Muchazo, tells him that she has spoken to her uncle who is looking for a tutor to help his son whose boarding school has shut down because of the war. The uncle who is a wealthy bus-line owner lives in Marimba Park, the suburb where the wealthiest Africans in the country live. The uncle has a two-bedroom servant's quarters which is vacant. The uncle needs someone to tutor his son, but he also needs someone to tend his flower garden and lawn. Andrew is excited and is willing to be a garden boy if this means that he has a home for himself and his father. In that same scene, however, Andrew is disappointed to learn that four of the band members have all left the country for Mozambique where they have gone to join the guerrilla army. He is even more disappointed to learn that Muchazo will be leaving the country too, to go study nursing in London on a full British Council scholarship.

The day after Andrew has started working at his new job, he goes to Rwizi's house to tell his father that he has found a job and a home for the two of them. But his father, old Majasi, is not there and Arimando, the house servant, does not know where he has gone to. Confused and worried, Andrew goes to Rwizi's office to ask him where their father is, he wants to take him to his new home.

Rwizi hems and haws and finally confesses to Andrew that he has placed their father in an old people's home in Plumtree, 300 miles away. Andrew is so upset he makes a scene in Rwizi's office. When he eventually cools down, Rwizi gives him bus fare to go get their father back from Plumtree.

In the next scene, Andrew holding his father's hat and a brown paper bag in his lap, is in Plumtree sitting by himself at a bus stop waiting for the bus back to Salisbury, crying. Two men destressed in military fatigues approach him and inquire why he is crying and ask if they can be of any help. Andrew tells them he is waiting for the bus to the city to go back to tell his brother that their father, Majasi, is dead. With tears in his eyes, he tells them that all that's left of his father are his personal items contained in the brown paper bag he is holding.

The two men express their condolences and reveal their identity to Andrew as freedom fighters who are operating in that area. They were already aware of the old man who died soon after he had arrived at the old people's home.

Andrew is sad but elated to have met the freedom fighters. He asks to join them. He believes their presence with him at that moment is a sign from his ancestors that now that his father is dead, he is free to go to Zambia or Mozambique to join the guerrilla armies fighting the Rhodesia Army.

The two men agree to take him to their training camp, but they tell him that he needs to bury his father first. They offer to help make the burial casket for him which will take at least a day. So, while they are making the casket, they tell Andrew, they want him to go back to Salisbury as planned to tell his brother about the death of their father. They want him to do them a favor by also carrying and delivering a package with him to an address in National African township. The package is a bomb.

Instructing him on how to carry it safely, they stress that even though the wires are not connected, he must not drop the package.

That night, Andrew, carrying the two packages in brown paper bags arrives back in the city and goes directly to his brother's house to tell him about their father's death. When he arrives at the house in Beatrice Cottages, he finds the house alive with music. Belinda and Sam are part of a tuxedo-and-gown well-dressed mixed crowd of whites, Indians, Coloureds, and Africans having a good time all being captured by a photographer.

Sally's ballroom dancing club party is on.

Dressed in a tuxedo, six-year-old John, who has been allowed to stay up late past bedtime that night because of the party, is the first to see his favorite uncle, Andrew, standing in the veranda. Excited to see Andrew, John comes to the veranda and tries to pull him into the house to join the party. Andrew tells John to go back and bring his father out to talk to him. Rwizi, who is tipsy, comes out happy to see his young brother, expecting to see his father in tow. Andrew delivers the sad news, accusing Rwizi of having sent their father to his death in Plumtree. Rwizi is devastated. He crumbles down on the stoep in the veranda crying, calling to his dead mother to forgive him for what he had done to his father. John, seeing his father crying, joins him on the floor, also crying and asking why his sekuru is dead.

Just before the presentation of the trophy, Sally, also tipsy from the champagne, sees Andrew standing on the veranda but does not see Rwizi and John slumped on the stoep. She slips out of the party to shoo Andrew away. She becomes particularly upset that Andrew, who had just travelled 600 miles round-trip, had shown up at her house during her moment of glory looking somewhat unkempt and poorly dressed. She is beside herself. She hisses at him, telling him to go away but Andrew talks back at her, telling her he will not allow her to treat him like she treats her houseboy, Arimando. A scuffle ensues. Rwizi, distraught, tells Sally to leave his brother alone.

Sally momentarily stops arguing with Andrew. She turns and is surprised to see her husband and son commiserating on the floor. She asks Rwizi what he and John are doing sitting on the stoep dirtying their new suits. Andrew tells Sally he is there to inform his brother that their father is dead. Sally is incensed. Accusing Andrew of spitefully coming and spoiling her party, she demands to know why he had chosen that moment that night when she was in the middle of her party to come and tell Rwizi that their father was dead. She yells at him to go away, telling him that she already knew that Majasi was dead and that she was going to tell Rwizi after the party. Hearing that Sally already knew that his father was dead and had chosen not to tell him, Rwizi is infuriated. He tells her to leave him alone so he can mourn his father.

Sally, determined to get rid of Andrew, pushes shooing him away. Andrew, holding the two paper bags loses his balance dropping the bag with his father's hat but manages to hold on to the bag with the bomb which lands on his chest. He lies still on the ground while Sally continues her drunken diatribe about Andrew's inconsiderate behaviour. Rwizi tells John to go to his bedroom and bring him his car keys and wallet and orders Sally to stop harassing his brother. He tells her to return to her party, which he was longer a part of. Sally asks John to come back to the party with her. John refuses to go with his mother, preferring to be outside with Uncle Andrew and his dad. Sally returns to the party alone. When John goes to get his father's car keys and wallet, Belinda follows him out of the party to find out what's going on.

Belinda sees the hat she had given Majasi laying on the ground along with Majasi's other personal effects scattered about from Andrew's fall, she asks why the hat is on the ground. Rwizi tells her that his father is dead. Belinda starts crying. She asks where Majasi is. Rwizi tells her he died in Plumtree; she is shocked and asks what he was doing in Plumtree. His response is, "Go ask your friend Sally, why my father died in Plumtree." He tells her he is not coming back to the party, he is driving to Plumtree with Andrew and John to collect his father's body. He is going to bury his father in Mhondoro next to his mother.

Epilogue

When the lights fade in, it is the last scene. The living room is empty. All the guests have left. Sam, who had been in the bathroom when the guests left, is holding Belinda in his arms unaware of what had transpired to clear the room and stop the party. Sally, holding the trophy, is sitting by herself on a chair, just shaking her head, not saying anything.

Sam asks, *Can someone please tell me what's happening. Sally, what's going on?* Sally does not answer Sams question. She appears to be in a daze, repeatedly talking to herself saying, *…that Andrew ruined everything, my guests just left my party, I didn't get to give my speech, the trophy was just handed to me with no ceremony, my picture won't be on the society page of Herald newspaper tomorrow, all because of that Andrew. He ruined everything.* She continues going on and on, lamenting how her party was ruined.

Getting no answer from Sally, Sam asks Belinda, what happened while he was in the bathroom?

Belinda responds and tells him she does not know but Rwizi said to ask Sally why his father was in Plumtree.

Sally continues talking to herself until she asks the empty room the question; *"Why did everyone just leave when the party was going on so well?"*

To which Belinda answers, *I told your guests that Rwizi's father, who I thought was sleeping in the bedroom, was dead. I told them Rwizi was not coming back to the party. That's why they left; it was not appropriate to be dancing in the house of a dead man.*

Belinda's response snaps Sally out of her daze as she declares, *But Rwizi's father is not dead in this house, he is dead in Plumtree.*

None of it is making any sense to Sam, who asks Sally why her husband's father is in Plumtree and why he died there.

Sally explains matter-of-factly that she found a facility for old people in Plumtree run by a fellow nurse matron and had Rwizi place his father there.

When Sam asks Sally why Rwizi would agree to put his father in such a desperate place meant for foreign Africans who have no family in this country.

Sally explains it all by saying, vaMajasi *did not belong here in our house. With his African ways, he was not a good influence on my son, John. We are a European cultured family. Didn't you see all the white people, Coloureds and Indians who came to our party? I wanted to have the championship party here in our house with people who are only like us. Rwizi's father did not belong here because he spoke in Shona in the house where I am teaching our son John to speak in English only. I told Rwizi he would be better off with other old Shona speaking Africans living somewhere else that's why I found him the place in Plumtree. Now it's all ruined because he is dead over there and Rwizi left me just as I knew he would if I had told him. That's why I had not told him that his father was dead.*

19

Belinda is shocked. She asks Sally, *What do you mean? You already knew that his father was dead? You knew it along?*

Calmly Sally responds, Yes, *my friend, Matron Katatu called and told me. He died two days ago.*

Belinda, incredulous, gasps, What?

To which Sally responds, *I was going to tell him tomorrow after the party. I just wanted our guests to have a good time at the party and have our pictures with this trophy in the newspaper. But that Andrew had to come tonight and tell him, just to spoil it for me. He ruined the only chance I had to show my white friends that we are not ordinary Africans. (Quietly sobbing) Oh my god no pictures in the newspaper.*

Belinda contemptuously shouts at her saying, *Never mind your pictures and your white so-called friends. Two days ago, you were told that your husband's father was dead. He died two days ago, and you didn't tell him? What is wrong with you? You don't see anything wrong with what you did?*

Sally is unflappable, she retorts, *What difference would it have made if I had told him then, his father was already dead? I know my husband; I know how he thinks. If I had told him his father was dead, he would have abandoned everything I have worked hard for to win the European classical music ballroom dancing championship as we did. He would have left me by myself, and I would have not won the championship trophy by myself because I dance best when I am with Rwizi. He knows how to move my body. Rwizi would have told me to get another ballroom dance partner and host this party all by myself. So, it was best to wait to tell him when I knew we would have time for funerals. Until now, we did not have time for*

20

that. It was about winning the Rhodesia Ballroom Dancing Association champion trophy and getting our pictures in the society pages of the newspapers. (She sobs)

Belinda ignores Sally's tears and tells her, *You are a mad woman. if you are ruined, it is your own fault. After throwing your father-in-law out of his own son's house because you wanted to have this silly party, you added insult to injury, by not to telling his son, your husband, that his father had been dead for two days. It is unconscionable that you sent that great man to his death like that. You are a professional medical person. Sekuru Majasi was not well. You knew that. He was the pillar of your family. You are a mad woman - to put away the pillar of your family just so you can have a party with these pretentious ballroom dancers and have your picture in the newspaper? Sally, you hardly know these people. See? Did any of them even express their condolences to you when they made a bee line out of your house? No. You know why? Because they do not know you and chances are they do not even care.*

Sally does not understand why Belinda is upset with her. She says, *Bee, you are talking like my husband now. It is not fair. You are blaming me for his father's death.*

To which Belinda says, *Sally the way you have acted, you might as well have put a pillow over his face and suffocated him to death yourself. Yes, your actions contributed to his death.*

As Sally protests that she did not kill Rwizi's father, she also realizes that her marriage maybe over, so she asks Belinda and Sam what she should do?

Sam admonishes her and tells her, *You better get yourself together and think about how you are going to make this right.*

Sally responds saying she does not know what to do.

Belinda, who is not feeling sorry for Sally, tells her, *First throw away that stupid ballroom dancing trophy you are holding. Throw it in the rubbish bin where your husband will never see it again. Follow him. You had better catch up with him and tell him you are sorry before he buries his father and your marriage with it.*

Sally continues to pity herself, bemoaning her fate saying, *I have ruined everything. I don't know what to do. I don't know what to do.*

But Belinda is not moved, she says, *"I am so upset with you and your obsession with all things European. I have a good mind to just leave you and your miserable pretend European life.*

Sam intervenes and tells Belinda, *No honey. You cannot just leave. She is your friend, we will drive to Plumtree with her and go to Mhondoro and help Rwizi bury his father.*

Belinda relents and tells Sally to change her clothes and find a dhoek to cover her head and a Zambia wraparound cloth for her dress for the funeral.

To which Sally says: *But I do not need a Zambia wraparound cloth, that's for poor women. I will wear that black dress. The civilized thing is to just wear black to a funeral.*

Belinda is exasperated.

She says, *Sally no, no, the black dress you are talking about is not long enough to wear to a funeral. It is not proper attire for a woman. It would be disrespectful in our traditional African society. (Shakes her head) I do not know any African woman in our country who doesn't have a Zambia wraparound cloth to go to funerals with. Well, I hope you have something to cover your head and I don't mean an English tea hat either.*

Sally assures her that she has a doek to cover my head.

Belinda ends the conversation saying, *Very well then, my husband and I are driving to Sekuru Majasi's funeral to honour him. He is our friend's father, and he was a great human being. And I am going there, to place his hat on his coffin because we loved him so. And, you, Sally, can do whatever you want.*

A cowering grateful Sally says, *I am coming with you. Thank you.*

CURTAIN

THE END

THE PLAY

CHARACTERS

Majasi: An old African man (Sekuru)

Rwizi: Majasi's older son (40ish)

Sally: Rwizi's wife (late 30s)

Belinda: Sally's friend (Auntie Bee)

Sam: Belinda's husband

John: Rwizi and Sally's 6-year-old son

Tino: John's friend same age (6yrs)

Andrew: Rwizi's 18-year-old brother

Arimando   Houseboy (servant)

Chaitezvi: Majasi's age mate and friend

Night Visitor: Old woman, Sally's aunt

Mbira Players: Chamu, Muchazo (Andrew's girlfriend) Max, Ticha, Tawanda & Zodwa

Mr. Mlambo: Neighborhood house homeowner

Political Activists: 7 African men and 2 women.

Comrades: 2 Freedom Fighters (guerrillas)

MC: James Goto, An African man

McIntyre: A white man

Photographer: A young man

Guests: Formally attired couples: white, Indian, Coloured (mixed race) & Africans.

HIGH CLASS NATIVES
Ballroom Dancers & Mbira Players

ACT One

Choto House - Evening

<u>Scene 1</u>

It is in the evening at Rwizi and Sally Choto's house in Beatrice Cottages, a petit-bourgeois enclave in the African Township of Harare, Rhodesia, circa 1977. What separates Beatrice Cottages from National, one of the City of Salisbury's African townships, wherein it's located, is that the houses in Beatrice Cottages are individually owned single homes with yards all around, a carport and a fence whereas the rest of the homes in that township are semidetached rentals owned by the municipal authority.

The action takes place in the dining/living room and the bedroom. The transition from one to the other will be effected using lights. Although Beatrice Cottages is something of an African middle-class enclave in Harare, the houses are just as small as those in the rest of the township. Thus, the dining/living room which occupies the greater part of the stage should be crowded with furniture without being over furnished. The background is dominated by a display case housing the crystal and china as well as a liquor cabinet squeezed in beside the display case, a stereo system in one corner and a bookshelf in the other. The centre should be dominated by a dining table with six chairs to match, the longish dining table and its chairs should be on a slightly raised platform, the foreground of the stage should have a living room suite consisting of a long sofa facing the audience, a love seat facing a television set placed beside a matching sofa under the window looking out of the room to a driveway. The kitchen is only suggested by a door and part of a stove which can be seen through the door. The bedroom is not an elaborate affair, there is a double bed a large mirror on a dresser and a closet full of clothes. The bathroom is not seen but suggested by a door.

Finally, there should be a veranda and a front door to the house centered towards the bedroom. The audience follows the action from a position directly across the narrow street that runs past the house.

LOUD MBIRA MUSIC OPENS THE SCENE IN DARKNESS.

When the lights fade in, the music dies down but continues to play in the background from a radio, MAJASI and his grandson, JOHN are seated on the long sofa in the living room. John, who is obviously more proficient in English, is struggling to tell his grandfather a story in Shona.

Majasi: Dzora volume, amai vako vakuya manje, manje. *(Turn down the volume on the radio, you mother should be coming now, now.)* John: *(Turns down the volume while talking to his grandfather.)* Ok.Ok. Now let me tell you a story. Once upon a time, there was a cow.

Majasi *(speaking deliberately in labored English)*: Shona, Shona purlize, me don'ti understendi Engirishi.

John: *(mixing Shona and English)* Okay, okay. Pange panhe cow. And then the cow yacho, ndobva yauya ….

Majasi: *(correcting him)*: mombe, cow izi mombe,

(Enter SALLY from the road, stage left. She is well dressed in a Harare Hospital Matron Nurse's uniform. Her cape and handbag are on her arm. She lingers at the door, eavesdropping on the conversation in the living room between John and his grandfather.)

John: Yes, yes. The cow yacho and then it came kah, and the cow cried mhuuu! mhuuu! mhuuu! and then ka, the lady wacho kah, started to run then the cow uhm, I do not remember the Shona words.

Majasi: *(The story is not making sense to him, but he nods his head enthusiastically)*: Uh, uh, uh,

John: And then kah, the cow yacho kah, I mean, mombe yacho ka.

Sally opens the door and enters the room. She stands, hands folded across her chest looking down at Majasi but speaking to her son, John.

Sally: John! What language are you speaking?

John: (*coyishly*): Shona.

Sally: How many times do I have to tell not to speak that horrible native language? How many times do I have to tell you to speak in English?

John: But I was telling sekuru (*grandfather*) a story and he doesn't understand English.

Sally: Never mind him. You must always speak English, Shona is for ignorant people, do you understand me?

John: Yes mum.

Sally: Now be a good boy, come and kiss mummy hello.

Sally leans down to receive the kiss. John ambles over and pecks her proffered cheek.

Sally: That's my baby.

Majasi observes the mother and son silently as if removed from the scene. He greets his daughter-in-law traditionally by slowly clapping his hands together as he greets her.

Majasi: (*in Shona*): Manheruka mukweguru. (*Good evening honored one*).

Sally: (*making no effort at tradition, she replies in English, still standing above him*): Good evening.

(*The lights dim out*)

Scene 2

(*Lights up in the bedroom.*)

Sally enters the bedroom closely followed by John. She throws her cape and handbag on the bed, takes off her shoes and opens the closet to find a dress, John sits on the bed.

> John: How come I didn't hear you drive up?

> Sally: Auntie Bee dropped me off because your father has the car. He drove into town to the tailor shop.

> John: You see, that's why you caught me speaking Shona. If you had driven up, I would have heard the car and I would have been speaking English only.

Sally finds a suitable dress and takes it down,

> Sally: Just remember what I told you. Do you want to be a kaffir?

> John: No.

> Sally: So, don't speak it then. Come and undo my zipper.

John obliges his mother.

> John: How come dad speaks it?

> Sally: You father only speaks it to ignorant people.

> John: He speaks it with sekuru, is sekuru ignorant?

Sally delivers her answer as she walks to the bathroom to change.

> Sally: Your father can speak it with his father if he wants to, but I don't want to hear you speak Shona.

Sally closes the door. John quietly opens the handbag and takes a quick peep at its contents. He closes the bag.

Sally returns to the room, changed into a stylish but comfortable dress.

John: Did you bring me anything?

Sally: Nothing for a bad boy, who speaks vernacular.

Sally sits on the bed in front of the mirror, combing her hair and generally admiring herself.

John: But I have been good.

Sally: Isn't mummy pretty?

John: Yes mummy, did you bring me anything?

Sally: How pretty is mummy, John?

John: You-are-the-prettiest-in-the-whole-world-did-you-bring-me-anything?

Sally: I said nothing for a bad boy.

John: But I have been good, honest, ask Arimando.

Sally: Where is Arimando?

John: He ran to the store to get your magazine. Please mummy, I promise, I will never ever speak Shona again.

Sally: You promise?

John: Yes.

Sally: Repeat after me, I am not,
John: I am not,
Sally: a monkey.

32

John: a monkey.
Sally: I will not speak Shona.
John: I will not speak Shona.

Sally: Good, now remember that. Look in my bag.

John opens the bag and finds a packet of sweets.

THERE IS A LOUD KNOCK ON THE DOOR.

Sally: John, go and see who is knocking at the door.

(Lights follow John back into the living room.)

Voice at the Door: It's me. Belinda.

John (*opening the door*): Hi Auntie Bee

BELINDA, a good-looking statuesque woman wearing the same Harare Hospital Matron Nurse uniform as Sally's comes into the room carrying an umbrella.

Belinda (*handing John the umbrella*): Hello handsome. Here is your mother's umbrella, she left it in my car. I had to come back with it because she may need it. I am off tomorrow, and it may rain.

Unlike Sally who stood over the old man Majasi when she entered the room, Belinda sits down and puts her hands together and claps them as she greets Majasi in Shona traditional greeting to an elder.

Belinda: Uh sekuru, makadhiyiko? (*How are you (sekuru) grandfather?*)

Majasi respectfully claps his hands back in response to the greeting.

33

Majasi: Tiripo, tino fara kukuonai. (*I am well, it is so good to see you.*)

Belinda: Kana neniwo ndinofara kukuonai makasimba. (*Me too, I am happy to see you looking well.*)

Belinda turns to John who standing beside her.

Belinda: John are you taking good care of your sekuru?

John: Yes, I am Auntie Bee. I tell him stories every day.

They all laugh.

Belinda: Ah nhai sekuru nziyo dzembira dzirikurira muradio dzakafanana here nembira dzekumusha. (*Sekuru are the mbira songs from the radio same as the ones you heard in the village?*)

Majasi: Eh dzakada kufanana asi ndajayira dzedu dzekumusha kwedu. (*Yes, they are similar, but I am used to our songs from the village.*)

Belinda: Ah motojaira sesu tinofarira mbira mumataundiship ano. Hakusisina kumusha ne hondo yapisa moto kumamisha yedu. (*There is nothing to do but to get used to it here in the townships as we who love mbira music do. Our villages are no longer there because of this the war raging in the countryside.*)

Majasi: Ndicho chokwadi Tete. (*That is the truth Auntie Bee.*)

Belinda (*stands up clapping*): John take good care of sekuru, when I come next time I will bring you some sweets.

John: Auntie Bee when you come, please also bring some Eat-One-Now biscuits for sekuru. Sekuru loves those biscuits.

Majasi shakes his head laughing.

> Belinda: That's all? No problem, I will bring yours and the biscuits for sekuru.

Belinda turns to Majasi.
> Belinda: Takuonai sekuru, handichagara. Ndagadauya ne umbrella yaMai John magwana kungagonaya. (*Sekuru I am not staying; I had just come to drop off Sally's umbrella in case it rains tomorrow.*)

> John: Bye Auntie Bee, I am going to give my mother the umbrella but do not forget my sweets.

> Belinda: I won't forget. Bye.

Belinda claps her hands respectfully to Majasi and leaves.
John goes back to the bedroom to give his mother the umbrella.

> (*The lights dim out*)

Scene 3

(Lights up in the living room)

Sally and John return to the living room. John tears the packet of sweets open and offers some to his grandfather, who takes one. Sally proceeds to the liquor cabinet and mixes herself a drink. She sits down in the loveseat facing the TV. Majasi is a silent figure sitting on the sofa facing the audience listening to the mbira music playing on the radio.

> Sally: John, turn off the radio. God, I hate that music. Turn on the teevee.

John gets up turns off the radio and turns the tv on. The volume on the tv is so low no one can hear anything coming from the tv. John starts to go out of the door.

Sally: Hey, where are you going?

John: Outside.

Sally: Come back and sit down. I don't want you going outside and playing with those dirty children next door. All they do is make monkey noises.

(John remains standing in the doorway.)

Sally: Come and sit down and watch tevee. You ought to be glad we have television in our house. Those children have no teevee in their houses, that's why they are such a nuisance.

John: I don't want to watch that boring Kiddies Program.

Sally: Your friends from school maybe on the program.

John: They are not my friends.

Sally: Yes, they are. You go to school with them.

John: They are white. Blacks are not allowed on teevee.

Sally: Don't say that be a good boy and come and sit down and watch tevee with mummie.

John reluctantly walks back into the room and sits on the sofa with his grandfather.

Enter ARIMANDO from the road, stage right. He is an African man in his twenties. He is dressed in a coarse khaki house-boy uniform. He opens the door and kneels in deference to his employer just inside the door.

Arimando: Gudhu evening medemu.

Sally: Good evening Arimando. I see you are empty-handed, where is my Scope magazine?

Arimando: They seidi thati it hazi noti kamu yeti.

Sally: Typical. Everything comes late to this godforsaken African township, civilization, magazines.

Arimando remains in his servile position on the floor. Sally sips her drink.

Sally: Well, don't just sit there. Go and prepare supper. We have ballroom practice tonight. Go on.

Arimando gets up and proceeds to the kitchen. As the scene unfolds the audience will be reminded of the cooking going on in the kitchen by the occasional rattle of pots and pans.

Sally: John, put some volume on the tevee. I don't want you to miss this.

John reaches the volume knob by stretching his body while sitting down on the sofa.

TV Voice (*with a British accent*) #1: And now children, today I am going to teach you a new game, I used to play this game when I was growing up in England, the name of the game is 'Backball'.
Now to play this game we must form a circle, make a circle. Come on, don't be shy, sit down, everybody.
What's your name young lady? Uh?
Oh, such adorable curls!
What's your name, don't be shy.

TV Voice # 2: Nancy McDonald

TV Voice # 1: Nancy. Good. You sit over here and everybody, come on children, and sit down in a circle beginning here, just like Nancy is. Good. The object of the game is to guess where I am going to hide the blackball, this rubber ball in my hand. You will all close your eyes. And I will hide it behind one of you. Are your eyes closed children?

TV Voices: Yes, Uncle Marty!!

TV Voice #1: Good. Good. Close your eyes. I am going to run around the circle and put the ball somewhere behind one of you. Close your eyes. No cheating. When I say open your eyes.

(*Fade TV volume*)

The sound of a car pulling into the driveway cuts Uncle Marty's voice on tv. The headlights of the car flash past the living room through the window looking out to the driveway John jumps to the sofa under the window beside the tv set excited.

John: Daddy is home! Daddy is home.

Sally: John! Sit down!

John does not respond to his mother's order.

John: But I want to see daddy drive into the yard.Oh, oh, daddy brought a visitor, mummy we have a visitor.

Sally: Stop jumping on my sofa. Come and sit down and learn the game Uncle Marty is teaching these nice children.

John climbs down from the sofa and goes to sit with his mother near the door. The sound of the car engine dies out.

TV Voice #1: Okay children. Let's start our game.

(*Fade out TV volume*)

The door opens.
Enter, RWIZI, a bespectacled 40-year-old African man. He is dressed in a
business suit and carries a briefcase. Close behind him is ANDREW, his young
brother. Andrew is 18 years old. He is dressed in a school blazer and a grey pair
of trousers. He is carrying a black metal trunk with his name, Andrew Choto and
school address, ST PAUL'S SEC SCHOOL -MSAMI written in brush white
across it.

John jumps at the sight of his father and hugs his legs.

    John: Daddy! Daddy!

    Sally: Rwizi, don't let him get all excited

    Rwizi: What have I done? All I did was walk into the house.

Andrew puts his trunk down while Rwizi turns to close the door. Andrew rushes
into the embrace of his father, Majasi.

    Majasi (*in Shona*): Mwana wemadzitateguru angu!
                Mupamombe!
                Vaka yambuka Zambezi
                Vari mudumbu remombe
                Baba vangu! Varidzi veRimuka
                Vema pipi
                Vavimhi vasina chavanotya
                Changamire!

Majasi and Andrew look into each other's eyes and laugh heartily.
John releases his father's legs from his hug. Rwizi puts his briefcase down and sits
with his wife.

    Rwizi (*to his father in Shona*): Manheruka baba (*Good evening*
    baba.)

Majasi: Manheru Mupamombe (*the father greets the son using their totem per Shona tradition*).

Andrew (*to John*): Hesi young man.

John: Hesi.

Andrew, unaware that Sally hates being spoken to in Shona in her house, greets her in Shona.

Andrew to Sally: How are you sister-in-law?

Sally (*stiffly*): Hello

Rwizi (*pointing to his briefcase*): Let me put this away.

Rwizi stands up with his briefcase and walks towards the bedroom.

(*The lights dim out*)

Scene 4

(*Lights up in the bedroom*)

Sally follows Rwizi into the bedroom. Rwizi takes off his jacket but keeps his tie on. He looks for an empty hanger in the closet.

Sally: Rwizi, what is the meaning of this?

Rwizi: The meaning of what?
Sally: You know what I am talking about.

Rwizi: Oh, your gown won't be ready until tomorrow.

Sally: Never mind my gown. What is the meaning of bringing that young man here without even bothering to inform me?

Rwizi: Andrew got off the bus from boarding school late this afternoon. He arrived at my office just before we closed. What was I supposed to do?

Sally: You could have called to tell me.

Rwizi: You didn't hear what I said, did you? He came to my office just before we closed. Which means you had already left the hospital? It is not as if we have a phone here in this house. Besides, Andrew is my younger brother.

Sally: Your brother or not, the house is already crowded, that is not to mention our permanent guest, your father.

Rwizi: What's the problem? We have three bedrooms in the house for Christ's sake!

Sally: Three bedrooms for us. You, me, and our son, John.

Rwizi: I am getting tired of this. You have been on about my father for a month now. What do you expect me to do?

Sally: You are getting tired? Uh?

Rwizi: Yes, I am getting tired.

Sally: I am the one who should be tired.

Rwizi: You are talking about my relatives.

Sally: So, what? You make them seem like some sacred objects. Relatives are people just like everyone else.

Rwizi: My father is not everyone else.

Sally: Every time I try to talk to you about this, you have gone off like a native barbarian. You should listen to me. We are civilized people. You and I are educated. We're a cultured family. We are not like those kaffirs who live in National. I don't see why you should act like one of them.

Rwizi: I am not acting like one of them.

Sally: Then why don't you listen to me with a level head. All I have been trying to do is help you see your way out of your problem. Our postal address maybe Harare African Township where they live like rats but as sure as I am standing here, we don't live in a location like National. We live in Beatrice Cottages, a suburb where modern, advanced, educated, civilized African people live. This is no place for people from the villages. I haven't asked you to throw your father out. Am I a cruel person? I am merely pointing out to you that unlike the old times in the villages, there are places for people like him. A place where he can be with people his own age, where they speak vernacular native languages and share the same interests.

Rwizi: I understand but can't you see that he is still in mourning. It is only six months since my mother was killed. The man not only lost his wife, but the Rhodesia government soldiers also burnt down his village. I saw what was left of it with my own eyes. It would be tough on any man. Surely you can understand that! (*Pause*) Anyway, even if I am going to make the arrangements you have been suggesting, don't you see that it should be after he has gotten over the death of his wife, my mother, and the loss of his home?

Sally (*not convinced*): That's all very well my darling, I don't have a mother or father, so I understand but I know old people, I see them every day at the hospital. Your father is not going to get over anything because even if he does get over it, he won't let anyone know about it. That way everybody feels sorry for him so he can manipulate us all.

Rwizi: But what can I do?

Sally: Take him where he belongs.

Rwizi: Besides the mourning, you know he is a sick man.

Sally: I am a trained professional. I should know a sick man. I brought your father that bottle of pills from the hospital, did he take even one of them? Anyway, they do have facilities for sick people there.

Rwizi: You don't understand. I am an African. Africans don't just do what you are asking me to.

Sally: No, you don't understand. Rwizi, you married me alone. You didn't pay lobola (bride price) because my life is my own, I am married to you, alone. Not to your father or your brother. You never heard me say a word when you used to drive our new car to that African reservation, Mhondoro, to see your relatives in the village, that was your affair. What I understand now is that you want to turn our home into a village for your relatives. If you insist on being an uncivilized African from there, you will leave me no choice but to say this. It's either you do the sensible thing, or you can live with him, your brother, and the rest of your village. They can all come here and make this house a hut. John and I will have to fend for ourselves elsewhere.

Rwizi: I don't believe you're saying that.

Sally: Oh yes, I am.

Rwizi: Well alright I will see what I can do.

Sally: No Rwizi. That won't do anymore. You are going to have to act and "not just see what you can do". I know how you just let things go without resolution, this is no time for that. I want to entertain our friends like we used to do. I can't do that anymore with him around.

Rwizi: Father doesn't get in the way. In fact, he hardly ever says anything.

Sally: He says a lot to my son and in Shona for that matter.
Rwizi: I will tell him not to.

Sally: That won't be necessary if you do the sensible thing. Remember the ballroom dancing regionals start this month, in another four months will be the finals, win or lose we are hosting the party after the dance here in this house. Our sophisticated friends, Whites, Indians, and Coloureds will all come to our house for the party, what will they think if your father is here? Where am I going to put all that furniture that's in the living room? It's bad enough that I must move most of my things from that spare room where he sleeps to John's, where will I put my furniture?

Rwizi: He could sleep in Arimando's room in the boy's kaya that night.

Sally: Armando's room? Armando's room is his own, he works for us.

Rwizi (*exasperated*): Alright, alright.

Sally: "Alright" is not going to do anything for anybody. And your brother Andrew, what are you going to do about him? He cannot possibly stay here. I must think about the welfare of our son even if you don't.

Rwizi: I can't send him to our village in Mhondoro reservation. Think about the soldiers - if they could kill my mother in cold blood like they did, what will they do to Andrew? Young as he is, they will accuse him of being a terrorist.

Sally: You know I drive to Mutoko to the mission schools to give them my donations of medicines and food. People still live in the villages. What is so special about your family if they have nothing to hide?

Rwizi: I will pretend I didn't hear that.
Sally: As you wish.

Rwizi: Andrew has just finished Form Four. I am sure he did well. He will get a job and find a place to rent, and father can live with him.

Sally: And in the meantime?

Rwizi: Couldn't he stay here for a little while?

Sally: A little while, uh? Your father came to stay for a little while six months ago. No, my husband. It is bad enough having your father around every day, it is impossible to have your brother as well. It has taken us all of John's six years to teach him to be civilized, to have some European culture. Your father behaves like a typical African from the bundu, undoing all my work of making our son a European. We send him to an expensive European school, and you expect me to sit back and watch your father drag him down to their level?

Rwizi: I can understand about father being unable to do things the way we have taught John, but Andrew is quite intelligent. He speaks English very well. It would be just a matter of telling him that we don't speak Shona in this house. I will make sure he behaves properly.

Sally: I do believe you think I am joking, don't you?

Rwizi: No, I can see you are serious.

Sally: Fine.

(Exit Sally)

Rwizi stares after her helplessly.

(The lights dim out)

Scene 5

(Lights up in the living room)

Sally enters the living room and makes herself another drink.
Andrew is talking to John.

Andrew: You are going to school like you are supposed to?

John: Yes.

Andrew: You like school?

John: Sometimes, but not all the time.
Andrew: Why not all the time?

John: Because some of the kids are mean, they pick on me, and gang up on me and call me names because I am black.

Andrew: Really? Do you fight back?

Sally (*intervenes*): John, I don't want you fighting anybody, do you understand?

John: But they pick on me.

Sally: They don't. You must play with those nice children.

John: Even when they beat me and call me kaffir?

Sally: They don't. You ought to be glad we found you a place in a European school.

Rwizi comes in and makes himself a drink and sits down.

Sally: Rwizi, tell your brother not to encourage my child to fight at school.

Andrew: I was only asking him about his school.

Sally: And telling him to fight with his white schoolmates.

Andrew: I...

Rwizi: John, have you been fighting at school?

John: No dad.

Rwizi: That's my boy. Come and sit here and tell me what you did today.

John jumps from the sofa and goes to sit in his father's lap.

Rwizi: Boy, you are getting heavy.

John: That's because I am big, and I can do the five times table.

Rwizi: Let me hear it.

John: Five times one is five, Five times two is ten, five times three is fifteen, Five times four is twenty, Five times five is, is, is... (counting on his fingers) five times five is thirty?

Rwizi: No that's five times six.

John: Yes, yes.

Arimando appears from the kitchen and kneels by the kitchen door.

Arimando: Medemu ken I si you ini the ketcheni?

Sally rises and follows Arimando to the kitchen, she stands at the door.

(The lights dim out)

(Spotlight Sally and Arimando at the kitchen door)

Arimando: I hevi finished cookingih, weya du I servi the vizita? (*Where do I serve the visitor's food?*)

Sally: Why, on the floor with the other visitor of course, he probably doesn't know the difference between a fork and a spoon.

(The spotlight dims out)

(Lights up in the living room)
John: Five times eleven is fifty-five, five times twelve is sixty!

Andrew: Wonderful.

Rwizi: My big man.

Sally delivers her chastisement as she retakes her seat.

Sally: Rwizi you act like you didn't know that John is a genius.

John: What is a genius?

Andrew laughs.

Sally (*to Andrew harshly*): It's not funny.

Andrew stops laughing.

Sally: John, a genius is someone very intelligent.

John: I am intelligent?

Sally: Of course, you know you are

John: But at school…

Sally: Never mind the school, go, and wash your hands, supper
    is ready.

John leaves the room to go and wash his hands.

*Arimando sets the table using the china and crystal ware from the display cabinet.
He sets bowls of food on the table. He returns to the kitchen and brings a tray with
two plates of food and a dish full of water and sets them on the floor in front of
Majasi. Sally, Rwizi and John sit at the table. Andrew and his father wash their
hands and proceed to eat their food from the two plates at their feet.
(At the table)*

Sally: They said my gown won't be ready until tomorrow?

Rwizi: Yes.

Sally: And your trousers?

Rwizi: They were ready, but I decided I would pick them up together with your gown.

Sally: You shouldn't have, I have that other gown I bought last year, of course it's a little too big now, seeing as how I have lost so much weight. I guess we'll just have to wear our old costumes for the rehearsal tonight.

Rwizi: I can't go to the rehearsal tonight. I must go to the meeting.

Sally: What meeting?

Rwizi: Party meeting.

Sally: Politics? Last week you went to another, tonight you are going again?

Rwizi: If I don't go, our house will be the only one not represented in the whole neighbourhood, it is just as well they haven't got around to asking us to host one.

Sally: Host one what?

Rwizi: The meeting venues rotate.

Sally: I won't have those kaffirs come into my house with their stinky ordours.
Rwizi: Don't worry honey, when I am asked, I will make excuses.

Sally: You say the whole neighbourhood attends? Are you telling me that Mr. Chikomo or Mr. Katoro, the secondary school headmaster attends those political meetings with all those uneducated people?

Rwizi: Yes.

Sally: They host meetings in their houses too?

Rwizi: I don't know. I haven't attended one in either of their houses.

Sally: There you are. People in Beatrice Cottages don't need these political meetings, they've better things to do with their houses, only those labourers and clerks, who live in National and other locations like that, have the time to waste with useless African politics. (*Shaking her head*) What these Africans need are people like me who drive to mission schools in Mutoko to give donations of food, medicines, and clothes. Not any of this politics foolishness.

They continue to eat in silence. However, Sally hardly eats. She stares at her husband who is avoiding her stare.

Sally: Rwizi, do you really mean to tell me that you are going to give up European classical ballroom dancing dress rehearsals to spend your time with a bunch of ignorant Africans howling at the moon and clamoring for independence from their white benefactors -shouting meaningless slogans about independence and majority rule?

Rwizi: Not all of them are uneducated.

Sally: What can you possibly get out of this?

Rwizi: You know, since mother was killed, I have had a lot of thoughts on the political situation in this country. If my mother had been a white woman, the soldier wouldn't have killed her in cold blood like that.

51

Sally: We were all deeply shocked by that, but you must realize that the soldiers were merely doing their duty. If she had not been mixed up with the terrorists none of this would have happened.

Andrew (*interjects*): She wasn't mixed up with anyone, the boys asked her to cook some meat which they had brought with them. What could she do?

Sally ignores Andrew's interruption.

Sally: Well, anyway, to get back to what I was saying to you Rwizi, you don't need to get mixed up with these people.

Rwizi: But what can I do?
Sally: What can you do? Don't attend, that's what you can do.

Rwizi: That is dangerous. They might think that we are sellouts.

Sally: Sellouts? Selling what? To who? What do they have in National that could be of any value to the Government? All those kaffirs shouting, 'one man, one vote' can't even speak proper English. They have too many children. Their wives are as dirty as their men who drink that, Rufaro Ngoto, that African home brew and fight in the municipality beer halls for my nurses to waste the hospital's valuable time stitching their empty heads. What can they do for you?

Rwizi: I must think of our safety as a family. If we are labelled Tsombes, sell-outs, unsympathetic to the black plight in the country, they could stone our house or our car when we're going to work.

Sally: So, you think you can protect us from their envy? The soldiers and the police will protect us, it's their job to protect us from these monkeys.

Rwizi: All the same I think it is my duty to go.

Sally: Sometimes you talk like little John here. Why don't you be reasonable? You think that these terrorists running around the countryside calling themselves Zanla or Zipra freedom fighters, guerrillas, whatever, will ever conquer the white man and take this country? You play with the power of Europeans. I saw it with my own eyes when I was in England. Imagine kaffirs talking about independence, majority rule -eh - you think that a black man like Mugabe or that fat one Nkomo can be a prime minister over white people? You play.

Rwizi: They have black prime ministers and presidents all over Africa, Kenya, Mozambique, Zambia, and Tanzania all over.

Sally: First of all, let me tell you this. They have black prime ministers and presidents over there because the white people didn't want to live there. Not like here in Rhodesia, the white people are not going anywhere. They are going to rule this country forever.

Sally poses, looking at Rwizi who is looking down eating his food.

Sally: And what are those countries anyway? Would you call Tanzania or Zambia a country? What do they have there, except hungry uncivilized Africans wallowing in poverty, lots and lots of it too? Africans in this country, this Rhodesia, would do well to count their blessings and thank God that Rhodesia is full of white people.

Andrew cannot stand it any longer.

Andrew: I don't see how there can be any blessings for the African to count under this white Rhodesia Front regime which kills and oppresses us all?

Sally: Oppress you? You must be full of that food that Arimando just served you. Oppress you? How does the white man oppress you when he built schools for you, when he gives you jobs? Without the white man would you have the clothes you have on your body?

Andrew: Yes.

Sally: This was a serious discussion between Rwizi and me. Don't interrupt unless you have something sensible to say.

Andrew: I am being sensible. You are implying that if it had not been for the Europeans who forcibly colonized us, the African would have become extinct.

Sally: I didn't say that. I asked you a simple question, without Europeans would you have the clothes that you wear?
Andrew: Maybe not this colour shirt. But yes, I would have clothes on, just as our forefathers had clothes to suit their environment. It might not have been synthetic material, but it served the purpose. The proof is that when we are left alone, we, Africans, do very well on our own. Our ancestors built the Great Zimbabwe with no help from any white man.

Sally: I am not talking about ancient history.

Andrew (speaking softly respectfully): Ok but *Mai Guru* (sister-in-law), you say Europeans are feeding us. True. They throw us the scraps from their table. Before they came, we had food which we farmed ourselves on our land and hunted from that same land. There are no blessings for the African to count in Rhodesia, there is only misery for us.

Sally: There is only misery for the lazy and uneducated. My husband is the assistant manager for the City of Salisbury

Revenue Department, and I am a matron at Harare General Hospital. We have done very well because of the white man and so have you.

Andrew: How can we do well when we are classified as not qualified to vote in our own country only because of the colour bar? How about our pride and dignity?

Sally: You don't need a vote to have dignity and pride. That comes from education and the clothes you wear. When I was in England, everybody was well dressed and educated. White people are really wonderful, that's what you Africans should be trying to do, be educated and wear nice clothes like white people, instead of biting the hand that is trying to feed you.

Andrew: Mai guru, you talk about England and yet you were there for only a month maybe...
Sally: So, I was there only a month, how many Africans do you personally know who have been to London or anywhere overseas for that matter, uh? Tell us?

Andrew: None.

Sally: So, don't argue with me about things you don't know anything about. The white man is trying to help you all.

Andrew: No mai guru, the white man is trying to help no one but himself. England for the English and Africa for Africans. Europeans should not come here and rule over us. That's tyranny not charity. They came with maxim guns and dynamite and killed our forefathers and forcibly grabbed everything we had for themselves.

Sally: Rwizi, you know your brother sounds like a communist terrorist?

Rwizi laughs.

Sally(*scornfully*): So, tell us Mr. Andrew Choto, what exactly do you have that the white man would want? What did he take from you?

Andrew: My country. Our land. We Africans owned this land collectively. We want it back and we are going to get it back. *Mai Guru* in Form Four they teach you the history of this country but if you read between the lines, you will see that Cecil Rhodes and Reverend Moffat were in cahoots to beguile King Lobengula, that's why Lobengula signed that fraudulent paper called the Rudd Concession which gave Rhodes the right to take over our country. It was a daylight robbery. We want our land back.

Sally: Your land? You have land in the African reservations and you blacks can't feed yourselves. You make me laugh.

Andrew: That's because it's poor soil.

Sally: You made the soil poor; that is why I keep telling you, you need education. With education you'd know that there's no such thing as poor soil in Rhodesia.

Rwizi: Eh, Sally I think you're being unfair to the Africans, granted they need education. But do you know that, that white farmer Danques who owns the store on Fort Vic Road owns more land on his farm by himself than all the land the government allocated for all the Africans in the Mhondoro African Reservation. So yes, I think it's only reasonable to say that these poor Africans could use some more land in the reservations. After all you can't plant and harvest from the same small piece of land over and over again. The soil dies.

Sally: More land to waste and make us all starve to death. I say no, let Danques and the rest of the European farmers have the land.

Andrew: Europeans are thieves.

They all laugh.

Sally: How childish, you don't have anything for anyone to steal, not even an African thief. What do you have?

Andrew: I am still young. I will get a job.

Sally: Yes, and don't you ever forget it. When you go to look for a job, you will be going to a white man. He will give you the job. He will put food in your mouth. He will put the clothes on your back.

Andrew: All that is going to change one day.

Sally: You really are one of them, aren't you? A terrorist, one of the communists. What party are you? Uh? ZAPU? ZANU? My God, my husband wasted our money paying for your school fees at St. Paul's. You don't appreciate anything, do you? (She mimics him) 'All that is going to change one day.' Let me give you some free advice, my boy. The only thing that is going to change is that the government is going to stop playing with you communists. When that happens, all of you are going to be thrown in jail where you all belong and the rest of your terrorist friends running around in the bush are going to bite speeding bullets. The government security forces will drag their dead bodies all over the land just as they did last week on tevee, when they killed that terrorist who was calling himself Comrade Mabhunu Mapera. He was the one that got finished not the white man. You can play with anything but do not try to play Ian Smith. There, you are now playing with fire. So here

57

is my free advice to you; Ian Smith said, 'Not in a thousand years. Africans will never rule this country.' You better believe it, not in a thousand years. So, stop wasting your time and make something of yourself with this education you have that my husband and I paid for.

John drops his fork loudly on the table.

Sally: John don't play with your food. Eat up...

John: But I am full.

Rwizi: Eat your food, John.

John reluctantly pokes into the food.

Sally: Honey, I hope you reconsider this meeting nonsense. None of these kaffirs have what we have, that's why they call you to meetings. They are envious, they'd like to see you arrested or something. We have white friends, a car, a nice house, television and our son goes to a European school where there are only six other Africans. You are already independent. You don't need majority rule in this country like these silly Africans are talking about. We already have majority rule in Rhodesia...(She turns to Andrew)
...as for you, young man, I should warn you to be very careful of what you say in front of my child. It costs us a lot of money to make him the good boy he is.

She drinks some water and leaves the table.

Sally (*shouts to the kitchen*): Arimando see that my old black evening dress is presentable. I am going to take a bath.

(*The lights dim out*)

Scene 6

(Lights up in the bedroom)

Sally has finished her bath and changed. She is putting on some make up. Rwizi is standing over her admiring her deft strokes with the eyebrow pencil.

Sally: I don't know what has come over you lately. You are being so stubborn. It's only 7:30 and we can still make it to the rehearsal together. We do have to win four regionals to make it to the championship, you know?

Rwizi: I know, we will be together on Saturday, so don't worry.

Sally: They may have some new entrance patterns, how are you going to learn them?

Rwizi: From you, the best dancer in the whole club.

Sally: I suppose you're right on that score. Anyway, I must leave now put John to bed before you leave.
Rwizi: Will do.

They kiss.

Sally: And Andrew, what're you going to do about him?

Rwizi: He can sleep in Arimando's room, can't he?

Sally: Ok but that room was built for one person, how many people can fit on that single bed?

Rwizi: He will sleep on the floor. The only other alternative is the hostels and as you know, over there it's twelve men to a room.

Sally: I know all that, but the fact remains, he can't stay here. I must think of the welfare of our child. Besides Arimando works for us, what does Andrew do for us?

Rwizi: You are not going to start that all over again, are you?

Sally: Very well.

Rwizi: I will find something for him in the morning.

Sally: Fine.

They both leave the bedroom followed by the light into the living room. Sally kisses her son goodnight and leaves.
With Sally out of the house, Rwizi and his father and brother, Andrew, speak to each other in Shona.

Rwizi: John are you ready for bed?

John: Can I watch teevee just a little?

Rwizi: No, no, I do not want to be late for my meeting, they have pungwe tonight.

John: But you always let me watch a little more teevee before you put me to bed.

Rwizi: I know, I know but not tonight. Nhasi kune pungwe.

John: What is "*pungwe* "?

Andrew: John pungwe is Shona, it means all night, until dawn.

John: So, will you be gone all night?

Rwizi: No, no I will leave when they start bhira?

Andrew: Bhira? What's going on over there mukoma (*big brother*)? Is it a political meeting, a social thing or religious something?

Rwizi: It's all those things. The meeting is hush, hush, Sally doesn't know it, but it was by special invitation which I accepted.

Rwizi continues to talk getting ready to pick up his son to take him to bed.

Rwizi: Yah it is a political meeting held under the guise of a bhira to make the government agents thinks we are just doing our African tribal rituals in case there is a raid.

Majasi: You said you said there's a bhira?

Rwizi: Yes baba, but the meeting is about the liberation of the country.
Majasi: Back at the village in Mhondoro Reserve wherever there was a bhira during school holidays, you were sure to find Andrew and his mbira.
Rwizi: Oh, how can I forget? I have not heard him play since forever. But I know Andrew was a child prodigy I bet now he is a mbira virtuoso. Over there where I am going, they play mbira mixed with electric guitars and drums. They call it mbira fusion to attract young people.

Majasi: It is a pity the soldiers burnt down his bedroom where his mbiras where stored the day they killed your mother.

Rwizi: Uhmm, such a pity.

Andrew: Do not worry, at least you, our father, survived the whole thing. I will make some new mbiras later when I am settled. So, mukoma can I tag along?

Rwizi: Considering the way you were arguing with your sister-in-law, you belong there.

They all laugh.

Majasi: She is just a woman. You know how they are. Let her get it off her chest and never argue with a woman. You never win.

Andrew: I didn't mean to argue with her.

Rwizi: I know.

Majasi: Andrew takes after me, he is head strong. Pride. (He chuckles to himself). Wilson, that's what they used to call me, and women, uh, what woman didn't want to marry me? Of course, our women were not like your women. They did not know how to speak English, but I could.

Andrew (*skeptically*): Uhmm baba really?

Majasi: Yes.

Andrew: Then what happened?

Majasi: I got old.

Laughter.

Andrew: No baba it doesn't happen that way.

Majasi: It does.

Rwizi: You expect I will be like you when I grow old.

Majasi: You better believe it.

Laughter again.

Rwizi: John, come on, get up.

It's bedtime.

Rwizi hoists John from the sofa and takes him to bed. He returns.

Rwizi: Arimando?

Arimando (*from the kitchen*): Sir

Rwizi: Andrew will sleep in your room. I am going to find a place of his own at the hostels later.

Arimando: Yes sir.

Rwizi (*to Andrew*): That's okay with you Andrew, isn't it?

Andrew: Yes, whatever you can fix for me, big brother.

Rwizi: Good. Now let me make sure John is in bed and we can leave.

CURTAIN

HIGH CLASS NATIVES
Ballroom Dancers & Mbira Players

ACT Two

Same evening at Mlambo's house

Mbira fusion music is coming from the house.
When the curtain opens, Rwizi and Andrew are arriving at the meeting venue. We
are at the Mlambo family residence. The setting is the same as Choto's house except
there is less furniture in the house. The action takes place in a living room large
enough to accommodate at least 12 people, sitting on the sofas along the wall and
on the floor. There is a coffee table in the middle. The door to the bedroom is visible
but closed.

Rwizi has an animal fur hat on his head, as he and Andrew enter Mlambo's
house. Mbira music is coming from the house. There are 2 young men sitting in the
verandah acting as lookouts.

Rwizi greets the two young men.

> Rwizi: Manheru machinda. (*Good evening, guys.*)

> Lookout #1 (*recognizing Rwizi*): Ah manheru mudhara. Pindayi
> zvenyu. (*Please enter sir.*)

> Rwizi: Ah ok. Uyu mufanha wangu, anonzi Andrew. (*This is my*
> *younger brother. His name is Andrew.*)

Andrew greets the 2 lookouts, shakes their hands and follows behind Rwizi.

Rwizi takes off his shoes, and so does Andrew leaving them outside the door where
other people's pairs of shoes abound. They enter the living room and find a place to
sit. In one corner are musicians playing traditional mbira music using various
instruments, mbiras, a guitar, drums, and percussions. Men with animal fur hats,
similar to Rwizi's, on their heads and women wearing wrap around cloth are
listening to the music clapping their hands to the rhythm of the beat. There are few
bottled beers being passed around. A beer is passed to Rwizi who waves it off and
so does Andrew. The music intensifies rising to a crescendo and gradually dies
down. MUCHAZOZVIONA (Muchazo), the lead singer, one of the mbira
players is a young woman about Andrew's age, her face is revealed when she puts
down the large gourd housing her mbira. Muchazo sees Andrew and their eyes lock

as she smiles at him shyly. Alongside Muchazo is CHAMUNORWA *(Chamu) the leader of the group also playing mbira. Chamu playfully nudges Muchazo in the ribs when he notices the silent interaction between Andrew and Muchazo.*

One of the men shouts: FREEDOM!

Everyone in the room: KWACHA

Rwizi: ONE MAN

Audience: ONE VOTE

One of women: MAJORITY RULE!

Everyone in the room: NOW!

The music starts again. There happens to be a mbira instrument laying on floor in the corner where the musicians are playing. Andrew gestures to Chamu that he wants to play that mbira that is laying on the floor. Chamu nods his head encouraging him to pick it up and come over and sit on the floor and jam with them. Andrew picks up the mbira and sits in with the musicians easily joining the rhythm of the song. Soon his virtuoso dexterity on the keys of the mbira takes him to the lead on the song and Muchazo abandons her mbira to focus on leading in the song with Chamu backing Andrew. The combination of Andrew's intensity and Muchazo's falsetto voice transforms the room into a traditional bhira. When the music finally dies down, Rwizi is the first to speak.

Rwizi (clapping his hands in traditional Shona greeting): Tiise maoko kuvadzimu veZimbabwe. (*Giving honor and thanks to the ancestors of Zimbabwe.*)

Everyone in the room: Tino tenda.

The door to the bedroom opens. Mr. Mlambo, a portly balding short man appears from the bedroom. He closes the door speaking as closes the door. Andrew returns to his seat next to Rwizi.

Mr. Mlambo: Ndanzwa izwi renyu vaChoto. (*I heard your voice Mr. Choto.*)

Rwizi: Hungu vaMlambo, tichangosvika wo. (*Oh yes. Mr. Mlambo, we have just   arrived.*)

The two men shake hands. Mr. Mlambo takes a seat in the corner that was clearly reserved for him. Someone hands him a beer. Which he accepts.

Rwizi puts his hands together and claps respectfully per Shona culture and speaks to Mr. Mlambo.

Rwizi introduces Andrew.

Rwizi: Takuudzirai gwenya mbira. (*Laughter*). Uyu ndiAndrew muningina wangu. Anga achifunda Form Four kwaMsami. Ato svikao nhasi. (*I brought you a mbira maestro. This is Andrew, my younger brother. He just arrived today from Msami where he was doing Form Four*).

Mr. Mlambo: Uhmm ndanzwa mbira dzacho nhasi dzine mhutinhi mbira wakasiyana. Tinofara Andrew chimbotiridzirayi Nemhamusasa titende vadzimu, hondo yauya. (*Uhmm I could tell there was a difference in the sound. Glad to meet you, Andrew. Play us Nemhamusasa so we can properly thank the ancestors, the war is upon us.*)

Andrew goes back to and picks up the mbira. They play the song, Nemhamusasa.

When the song dies down. Rwizi speaks.

Rwizi: Tino tenda kuonana. Mabasa akadhiyiko? (*We are grateful to see each other. How have you been?*)

Mr. Mlambo: Tafara makwanisa kuti shanyira. Zvinhu zvaoma. (*We are delighted that you were able to come visit us. Things have become hard.*)

Rwizi: Hondo yatanga kuvaruma varungu. Tazviona mutown nemuma offices, vakanyarara. Zvinhu zvavakuchinga. (*The war is beginning to bite white people. We see it in town and in our offices. They are awfully quiet these days. Things are changing.)*

Mr. Mlambo: Hongu tongo ramba takatsigira vakomana nevasikana vari kuti rwira hondo yedu. (*Yes, but we must remain steadfast and continue to support our boys and girls in the bush, fighting this war for us.*)

Rwizi reaches in his pocket and takes out some money (dollars) and gives it to Andrew to pass on to Mr. Mlambo. Mr. Mlambo accepts the money.

Mr. Mlambo (in Shona): Thank you, money is most convenient to help support them. Someone left a bag of clothes and shoes at my store. There are good clothes, jeans and canvas shoes the boys need them but if I had been in the store, I would not have accepted the bag because it's difficult for our couriers to move around with bags of clothes with all these informers and roads blocks all over the place.

Rwizi claps his hands and asks to be excused to return home.

Rwizi: Ini handichagara. Ndangandago uya necontribution yangu. Magwana kubasa. Andrew anga sare zvake achitandara nemi muzivane. (*I am not staying any longer, I had just come to give my contribution. Tomorrow is a workday. Andrews can stay and continue with you all, so you may get to know each other.*)

Mr. Mlambo: Pakanaka vaChoto. Tinotenda necontribution dzamunoita. Dzino batsira chaizvo. (*Very well Mr. Choto. We thank you for the contributions you make. It makes a big difference*).

Rwizi: Munotendeyi? I hondo venyika yedu. (*There is nothing to thank me for. It's for the struggle for our country.*)

As Rwizi leaves. The musicians launch into another song.

CURTAIN

HIGH CLASS NATIVES
Ballroom Dancers & Mbira Players

ACT Three

Choto House - Three months later - daytime

<u>Scene 1</u>

It is afternoon on a Friday at Choto's house. The action takes place on the veranda which faces the narrow-tarred street that runs past the house. There is a low chain link fence with a gate in front of the house part of which can be seen by the audience. There is a small green lawn between the fence and the veranda, running the length of the house. The portion of the veranda seen by the audience is to the left side of the front door with a window which looks into the dining/sitting room. Since the action is outside there will need to be some ambient noise from the neighbourhood, the street and neighbours passing by.

When the scene opens, six-year-old John is racing a toy car on the floor of the veranda while his grandfather, Majasi, is sitting in a chair facing the street. Although it's nice and sunny weather outside, Majasi is wearing an overcoat talking to his grandson enjoying mbira music coming from the radio inside the house.

John (*talking to his grandfather without looking up at him*): Sekuru how come you like that mbira music so much?

Majasi: Ndiyo manzi yedu yechinyakare ka. *(It's our traditional music from chinyakare time).*

John: Sekuru what is "chinyakare"?

Majasi: Chinyakare means kubvira kudharadhara. *(It means from an old time long, long ago).*

John: Are you chinyakare?

Majasi (*guffaws*): No, I am not that old. It means a long time even before I was born.

John: Ah you see sekuru, you speak English!

Majasi: Me, I dondi I understandi Engilish.

72

John: Ah sekuru, I know you now, you just pretend. I know you understand English.

Majasi (laughing): Newe futi ndinokuziva. Unogona Shona futi. (*And I also know you. You know Shona too.*)

John: But sekuru if you can speak English how come you always want to speak to me in Shona?

Majasi: Ndirwo rurimi rwedu ka. (*Because it is our native language.*)

John: But my mother says Shona is for ignorant people. Are you are ignorant?

Majasi: Ko iwe unofungeyi nazvo? (*What do you think?*)

John: No, you are not ignorant. You are my best friend. *(He stands and hugs his grandfather).*

Majasi:(*laughing and hugging John speaking in English):* Of course, I can speak English but why should I? English people have their own English language. African people have their own African languages. Shona is my African language. So, I only speak English when I feel like it. And you should be like me, learn to speak English, Shona, Ndebele…all our languages. You understand? Language is for talking to people not for kuvhayira.

John: What is kuvhayira?

Majasi. Bragging.

John: Sekuru what is bragging?
Majasi: Bragging is to show off, to act like you are more important than other people? It's not good.

John (*nods his head in agreement*): Yes. Kuvhayira is not good. Sometimes my friends laugh at me when I speak Shona. They say I speak English, Shona but I don't care. I like playing with my friends.

Majasi: Very good.

John goes back to playing with his toy.

John: Sekuru, I am hungry, where is Uncle Andrew?

Majasi: Arikuuya manje manje. (*He will be here anytime now.*)

John: I wish he would come now, now because when mother is not here to tell Arimando to give us lunch, Arimando just waits to cook until he thinks we are all here.

Majasi: Baba mudhiki vako varikusvika manje manje. (*Your uncle will be here soon.*)

Majasi starts nodding his head to the beat of the mbira music coming from the radio.

Majasi: Isa volume muradio. Ndinoda rwumbo rwuri kurira. (*Go and turn up the radio. I love that song*).

John runs into the house to turn up the volume of the radio.

While John is in the house, Andrew arrives from the street, opens the gate and walks to the veranda where his father is sitting. He greets his father clapping his hands per tradition standing by the door about to enter the house. Majasi and Andrew speak to each other in Shona.

Andrew: Regai nditore chair. (*Let me get a chair*).
He enters the house and returns to the veranda with the chair and sits down.

Andrew: Masikati Mupamombe, kokupfeka overcoat kuchidziya, idhava? (*Good afternoon Mupamombe. Why the overcoat in this warm weather?*)

Majasi: Zvedu zvechembere zvino tevedzerwa here? Ndine kachando nekungo dzimbwa dzimbwa. (*Ah never mind me. I have a little chill and little body aches. It's just old age.*)

Andrew: Alright. Pakanaka kana madharo. (*Alright if you say so.*)

Majasi: Ndimika vavhimi vemaindustry. Masango akamira seyi Mupamombe? (*So, tell me Mupamombe, you are the hunter. Tell me how the hunt is going out there in the wild forests of businesses and industries?*)

Andrew (*sounding dejected*): Baba kwapera mwedzi 3 ndichingo tsvanga basa. Hakuna kana kajob kana. (*Ah baba it's been three months! For three months I have been job hunting! There is nothing, nothing out there. Nothing.*)

Majasi (*nodding his head sympathetically*): Hongu ndiri kuzvinzwa asika mwanangu mwedzi mitatu haasi makore matatu ka. (*Yes, I hear you my son, but three months is not three years.*)

John returns to the veranda.

John (excited hugging Andrew): Uncle Andrew! I was in the bathroom, so I did not see you come in. I have been waiting for you! What took you so long to come today? Aren't you hungry? I am hungry. Did you know that Sekuru can speak English?

Andrew: Woaw, woaw slow down little Mupamombe, slow down. First you must greet me properly like I taught you.
John: Ok. Ok.

Majasi and Andrew with smiles on their faces, watch John take a step back and get into a traditional squat position and put his little hands together.

John (*claps his hands as he speaks in Shona*): Masikati Mupamombe. (*Good afternoon Mupamombe.*)

Andrew (*laughing approvingly*): Masikati Mupamombe. You did good John. Now get up, come, and sit with me while I talk to Sekuru.

John gets up and joins his grandfather and uncle.
Arimando brings a dish of water and food on a tray and places them at their feet.

Arimando (*in broken English*): John kamu ini-seidi the house and sit at thi teburu.

John: I want to eat here on the veranda from the floor like Sekuru and Uncle Andrew. Can I?

Arimando: No.

John: Why not?

Arimando (*in broken English*): Bekozi your matha seyi you all wezi eat at thi teburu.

John: Uncle Andrew, can I wash my hands and eat from your plate?

Arimando (*in broken English*): No John, camu or I wiri teri your matha.

John: Please uncle. I hate that table. I wish we did not have a dining table.

Andrew: No John. You are a Mupamombe. You listen to Arimando. Now go and eat at the table before we all get into trouble with your mother.

John sulks but follows the order and goes inside the house.

Majasi and Andrew eat from the floor. They continue their conversation in Shona.

Majasi: You don't look well my son, you're all skin and bones.

Andrew: You do not look so good yourself, baba.

Majasi (shrugs his shoulders): Uhmm.

Andrew: It's tough out there in the job market baba.

Majasi: I know, Mupamombe. But what can you do, except keep trying?

Andrew: If it was only one thing, it would not be so hard. As it is, just staying one foot ahead of the police is a job in itself.

Majasi: Uhm?

Andrew: If you are unemployed, you're a vagrant and yet to get the jobs you have to go and hang around outside the factory gates and places like that where employers pick up the lucky ones. But the police come and arrest you there too, the same place where you go to look for work to be employed so that you are not a vagrant. I don't know.

Majasi: It is all right son; you'll find a job someday.
Andrew: Until then, where do I stay? What do I eat?
Majasi: You are a man, my son, you will stay in the hostels and eat here as you have been doing since you came from boarding school.

Andrew: Baba, even if I wanted to, there is no place for me to cook over there but besides that I have no money to buy anything to cook and no pots to cook the nothing I have in. So here I am. Everyday lunch time, if I do not want to starve to death, I must trudge five miles from Matapi Hostel to come here to Beatrice Cottages to eat and trudge back five miles, by the time I get back, I am as hungry as I was when I left. I live in a room with nine men, older than my brother, Rwizi. There are so many thieves and muggers that no one keeps any clothes in the room except maybe their underwear but that can get stolen too. They steal teaspoons, can you imagine that? A teaspoon? And then of course there is the police. We hardly ever sleep in peace. They come at all hours of the night. 'stupa'' stupa' as if a stupa is life. Sometimes I wonder about it all. I am sure that when I was born, this was not your plan for me.

Majasi reaches into the folds of his coat and gives Andrew a $2 note.

Andrew: Thank you baba.

Majasi: I know sometimes the struggles in life may seem impossible, especially in times of hardship like you are going through now. However, you are still young. With age you gain patience and the knowledge that to all seasons, there is a turn. Right now, it may seem like it is winter in your life, but winter always turns to summer. Nothing good or bad lasts forever. Bide your time my son. Let's be thankful to our ancestors that we have your brother who can take care of us as he has done.

They eat in silence.

Majasi: I don't know what the spirits of our ancestors here in this Rhodesia have in store for us. This horror has gone far enough. I don't know what God did to our country. It is almost as if he has decided to give it to the white people forever.

Andrew: Others of my age are crossing the border to take up arms, to join the guerrilla armies in Mozambique and Zambia to fight these white people and their leader Smith to stop this horrible system of government. Sometimes I think killing them like they are killing us is the only solution.

Majasi: So, it might be, but if you go, what will happen to me? Your mother is dead, if she was still alive maybe I would be well myself, but she is gone, you are the only one left and I am a sick old man.

Andrew: Baba, I didn't say I was going to go and join the freedom fighters. It's just talk, Mupamombe, it's just conversation.

Majasi: Contemplating vengeance for your mother's death will not help anything. I have lost much more than that and so have most Africans my age. Let it be my son, don't go. Our ancestors will look after us.

Andrew: It is just talk Mupamombe, I am not going.

Majasi: Yes, my son. I know you would not leave me. You will find a job. Your mother is gone. She is where she can look after you and help you find one.

Andrew: Maybe I am having all this bad luck, not finding a job because mother's family did not perform the rituals for her spirit. Maybe that's why I haven't been able to find a job. Maybe her spirit is restless.
Majasi: Who knows? You may be right, the spirits of Zimbabwe are disturbed and there is nothing anyone can do,

Andrew: Surely something can be done.

TINO, a boy about John's age appears outside the fence and shouts.

Tino: Sekuru where is John? We are playing soccer.

Before Majasi can open his mouth to respond, John suddenly appears at the door and shouts back at the boy.

John: Alright Tino, I am coming.

Andrew: John, did you finish eating?

John: Yes uncle, honest, ask Arimando.

Andrew: Ok but come back before I leave.

John: Ok I will come back soon, soon.

John leaves.

Andrew and Majasi continue their conversation.

Andrew: Baba I have been thinking. As I was saying, maybe I am having bad luck finding a job because my mother's spirit is not at rest. Maybe it is because we have not done the rituals.

Majasi: My son, your mother is not of our bloodline. We cannot do the rituals for your mother. Only her family, the people where she came from, they are the only ones who can do it for her because she is their daughter.

Andrew: But maybe they do not know what I am going through. We should send a word to their village and tell them to get together and perform the rites and rituals to help my mother's spirit find peace so she can help me.

Majasi: Where, in that village, are her people going to perform the rituals to help you and how? No one is allowed to assemble in large numbers in the villages anymore. Besides a lot of

80

people from her family have been forcibly moved to the "keeps". You know? Have you been to one? They call these keeps protected villages. But there is nothing village like about them. They are actually just high wire fenced camps of shacks built from metal sheets by the government. They have soldiers on guard everywhere to prevent the people from moving freely. The government is afraid people will supply our boys with food. On top of that the government has imposed a dawn to dusk curfew over there. So, if you cannot bring people together at night, how are you going to perform the rituals? The villages are death camps nowadays. If you do any rituals and the soldiers catch you performing them, they will accuse you of praying and giving magic to the guerrillas to defeat Smith and his soldiers. Just on that suspicion, they will shoot you like a dog. You know how they are.

John suddenly returns running almost out of breath.

John (shouting): Sekuru, sekuru, sekuru. I have a secret to tell you.

Andrew: If you are shouting it out loud like that, then it's not a secret.

John: It is too, a secret. It is a secret, and I am only telling my friend Sekuru.

Majasi: Come whisper in my ear muzukuru (grandson).
John goes around Andrew and whispers in his grandfather's ear.
Majasi bursts out laughing.

Andrew: What's the secret? What's so funny?

John: Uncle Andrew, you better get ready.

Andrew: Ready for what?

81

Majasi is thoroughly amused.

Majasi (laughing): He says you have a girlfriend.

Andrew: What?

John: Yes, I saw you holding hands with a girl.

Andrew: What girl?

John: The one that's coming down the street. I saw her from the playground where we are playing soccer. She is coming.

Suddenly Andrew asks to be excused and scabbles up and takes the food tray into the house.

Andrew: Baba let me go in and wash my hands in the bathroom.

Majasi is in stitches laughing at Andrew.

Tino, John's friend, followed John to his house.

Tino (*leaning against the fence*): John hurry back, we have no goalkeeper?

John: E-her I am coming.
John follows his friend and leaves.

A bashful Andrew returns to the veranda resumes his seat.

Majasi: Uhmm you look different...you are smiling. I guess it's true.
Andrew: What?

A young man, CHAMUNORWA (Chamu), and young woman,
MUCHAZOZVIONA (Muchazo), both around Andrew's age come into the
view on the street about to pass the Choto house. They see Andrew and stop and
greet each other. Chamu carrying a mbira and Muchazo carrying 2 mbiras briefly
lean against the fence.

Chamu: Andrew!

Andrew: Hi Chamu, hi Muchazo, how are you?

Muchazo seems shy and uncomfortable. She looks down as she speaks so softly no
one can hear what she said.
Andrew stands and waves them to come in.

Andrew: Come into the yard and say hello to my father.

Chamu and Muchazo enter and come to the veranda. Andrew gives his seat to
Chamu, and he sits on the floor at the edge of the veranda and Muchazo sits on the
grass. Chamu and Muchazo put their mbiras down.
Andrew is a bit nervous. He clears his throat. The conversation is in Shona.

Andrew: Baba these are my friends, Chamunorwa and
Muchazozviona: people this is Mupamombe, my father.

Chamu and Muchazo (clap their hands in respect): We are
pleased to meet you Mupamombe.

Majasi: I am happy to know you, my children.

Andrew: On your way to practice?

Chamu: Yes, we are going to practice. We thought you would
be there already.

Andrew: I was just finishing visiting with my father.

Majasi sits up:

Majasi: So, you both play mbira?

Chamu: Yes sir. We both do and Andrew too.

Majasi: Uhmm. Andrew did not tell me he has friends who play mbira. You know Andrew has been playing the mbira since he was as young as his nephew John. He is a virtuoso. I taught him myself.

Chamu: Yah baba we know Andrew can play, he has even taught me a few things to change the way my keys sound.

Majasi turns to Andrew.

Majasi: Andrew, I am happy you are not all alone, my son. A young man needs to be around other young men. This city of Salisbury is a jungle, people here in the city do not know each other. At home in Mhondoro you had many, many friends. You are well known for your mbira skills. Where did you meet your friends?

Andrew: We met that night when I came back from Msami. That time when I went to that meeting with my brother Rwizi.

Majasi: Oh yes, your brother mentioned that there would be a bhira there. So, are you the mbira players for the bhira?

Chamu: Yes, sir. There is only six of us now, but we will be seven   and a complete band if Andrew can join us more often.

Majasi: But why didn't you tell me Andrew that you have friends like this who do what you like?

84

Andrew: I have been playing with them sometime when I can. But most of the time, I am too tired because of all the time I spend walking in the industrial sites looking for a job.

Majasi is taken by the quiet girl sitting on the grass before him.

Majasi *(jokingly)*: Uhmm young lady, you are so quiet, like a muroora *(daughter-in-law)* visiting her in-laws. (*He laughs*) So it is true what John said that you are my muroora?

Muchazo is embarrassed. She keeps her head down smiling.

Andrew *(embarrassed)*: Ah baba.

Chamu *(laughing)*: Yes, it is true baba. She is your muroora.

Majasi: Ah really that is very good.

Andrew: Chamu! I thought we were friends, what's wrong with you?

They all laugh except Muchazo who keeps her head down.

Majasi: So, tell me, muroora, where are you from?

Muchazo: Uhmm my father is from Chiweshe, but I was born here in Harare, in National.

Majasi: And what is your totem.

Muchazo: Soko

Majasi: Ah that's good, Soko and Mupamombe can go together.

Chamu (*laughing*): That's good! It makes my job easier. I am the munyayi. I am the go-between, the marriage negotiator.

Muchazo keeps her head down. Andrew is embarrassed.

Andrew: Baba please. Chamu, will you stop it!!

Chamu (*laughing*): Stop what? I am just doing my job.

Majasi: It is all in jest, you are all still young but not too young. And of course, with the uncertainty of the times, you never know. So, what about school, are you like Andrew. He was very good in school, he finished Form Four, but the way things are going you would think his Form Four was a waste of time and money. The jobs they have for Africans these days... uhh. (*Disgusted*)

Andrew: Baba, I will take any job they offer me. Even though I have my Form Four education I am now at that point where I am willing to sweep the streets, sell tomatoes, clean toilets. I am even willing to carry bags for white people. I do not care anymore I just want a job I need money to take care of you.

Andrew points to Chamu.

Andrew: Baba this funny guy, Chamu, you see here full of jokes, he finished Form Six. He passed his A levels.

Chamu: Oh yes Mupamombe, I have A levels. I was hoping to go to study to become a lawyer, but things are tough, everything is upside down in Rhodesia.

Majasi: And how about you muroora?

Muchazo *(confidently raises her head for the first time and responds):* I completed my "O levels" too. Maybe if I get a place, I want to go to London to study nursing.

Majasi: So, you are all just waiting for something?

Chamu: My problem is they want me for "call up" duty. The government is losing the war to the guerrillas, they need more bodies. Remember because of the colour bar the Rhodesia Army has just been for white people, Indians and Coloureds *(mixed race)* only.

Andrew *(with a fake Rhodesian coloured person's slang & accent):* Don't tune me grief exse. Me, I'm not gonna be in no Rhodie Army. I'm no longer Coloured, I don't come from Arcadia no more. I am now an African from Wedza African Reservation! I aint gonna fight them communist ters for Smith!

They are all laughing at Andrew's poor imitation of a Coloured person's accent. Chamu jumps in with a fake British accent.

Chamu: Andrew old chap. I am taking the gap (leaving the country in a hurry). These commie goons mean business. I saw it happen in Kenya with Mau Mau, I left. I saw it happen in Zambia, I left. Good old Smith is a nice chap but, it is here now. Rhodesia is finished. I am leaving. I am off to South Africa now. White people are doing very well in that apartheid system they have down there. Besides, they have nice British clubs over there and great vineyards too. I love South African pinot noir.

Andrew is in stitches laughing, he jumps in.

Andrew: My good man what's gonna happen to your wonderful British pinot noir ass when the ANC and PAC commie goons come knocking on your swanky white apartheid door in South Africa!

Chamu: (*still in his fake British accent*): Never fear old chap. Australia here I come, like America, in Australia, we got rid of the natives. Over there, the natives are mostly dead. Not like these natives here in Africa, they are too much trouble, you kill one, here comes another and they do not stay dead.

They all fall out laughing.

Chamu: But seriously baba, I am not going to call up. They will have to catch me first. I am not going to fight my own brothers and sisters to benefit white privileged Rhodesians. If I must go for national call up duty as part of the conditions to enroll in the law degree program at the university, then I would rather not go even though I have been dreaming of becoming a lawyer since I can ever remember. I do not care. I would rather just play my mbira. I won't starve.

Majasi: But Andrew, my son, you joke about some Coloureds changing saying they are not from Acadia but Wedza, it is true. You have light skinned Africans who changed their names to European names to enjoy white privileges in Rhodesia. But there are just black people like us passing for Coloured.

Andrew (*jumping in*): Baba it would be a foolish thing if I went for call up like that. I say let them call up the Coloureds to join the whites and Indians to go face the terrorists. I am not a Coloured! I have nothing to defend. I have never enjoyed the privileges the coloured have to get jobs at the post office or apprenticeships at the railways. If I was a Coloured, I would not be in this hopeless jobless situation I am in now.

Chamu: If you need a job that bad, it is not too late. Muchazo can run a hot comb through your kinky African hair and make

88

it straight to lie down on your head to look like a black white man. You already got the fake Coloured accent, I have heard worse. All you need now is to go register and get an id as a Coloured under the name something, something Andrews.

Muchazo: As soon as you register as a Coloured they will be waiting for you to conscript you into the Rhodesia Army.

Chamu: Ah that is no problem. You just do a tour of duty and come back they will give you an apprenticeship at the railways.

Andrew: That is "if" I came back. Not me, I do not want to come back in a body bag.

Majasi: Eiie things are tough for your generation nowadays my children. It was not so hard for us. When I was your age, I came from our village in Mhondoro African reservation after some schooling and in no time, I got a job as a clerk at the Costain Company.

Andrew: Really baba. I did not know that.

Majasi: Ah yes, I came and worked here but just long enough to save money to buy some cattle to marry your mother. Then I went back. I lived in Old Bricks.

Chamu: Mupamombe you were at clerk at Costain? Was it a big company then?

Majasi: I do not remember how big it was but there were a lot of workers. They were always hiring people to work there.

Chamu: Well, Costain is no more. They closed.

Majasi: Uhmm what happened? They were a good company - many, many things sold in the stores in town were manufactured at Costain.

Chamu: Sanctions baba. Sanctions. Rhodesia is now reeling under United Nations economic sanctions because this minority white government will not share democracy with us, the black majority. Costain company is one of the companies that have become casualties of the sanctions. The company was no longer able to import the raw materials they needed to operate the business, so they went bankrupt.

Majasi: Ahh it's such a pity. It was a good company. The white people there treated us well. Ah well, but it is good if white people lose their businesses and money too because of sanctions. So, they suffer too, like we are suffering.

Andrew: But baba, that's one of the reasons why I cannot find a job.

Majasi: Uhmm nothing we can do.

Chamu touches the keys on his mbira.

Majasi: So, Andrew, when shall I hear you play mbira again. The way you play mbira makes me come alive.

Chamu calls Muchazo.

Chamu: Hey, Muchazo, maybe this a good time to give Andrew his mbira.

Muchazo hands Andrew one of the two mbiras she was carrying. Andrew is totally surprised.

Andrew: Really? Oh, my ancestors. Really? Baba, do you see what they have given me? How do we thank you?
Muchazo: We all contributed, Max, Ticha, Tawanda, Zodwa, me and Chamu, all the band members. We got it for you.

Chamu: You cannot be a full member of a band if you have no mbira of your own, right baba?

Majasi: This is a great thing my children. A really great thing. This is friendship. That is how it is done. We thank you.

Chamu: It is nothing baba. Andrew is a great mbira player. We want him to play with us. This is a small token of our admiration of his skill as a player and teacher.

Andrew: Baba if things keep going the way they are going, I might as well join Chamu and Muchazo in the mbira band.

Majasi: What is the name of your mbira group?

Chamu: Zi-Mbira Band

Andrew: Baba he means, Zimbabwe Mbira Band.

Chamu: Yes. But here in Rhodesia you can't use the word Zimbabwe on anything. If you do, the CID will take a very special interest in you. And we do not want to go to jail call up.

Andrew laughs.

Andrew: Jail call up? We may end up in there anyway with the kind of songs you make up.

Chamu: Ah it's a chance we should take. Look at Thomas Mapfumo. He is doing quite well with his Chimurenga songs and people buy his records like crazy, even overseas.

Majasi: Ah Thomas, that Mukanya has a special gift. He takes our Shona traditional songs and puts guitars and mbira in

91

them, and it sounds so good even us old ones enjoy our old traditional music like it is new. I am happy that our traditional music is not dead because young people are using it to inspire the fight for our freedom in Rhodesia.

Andrew: Baba you are so right. Thomas is now an international music star. I think even though the CID Special Branch harasses him because he sings about Zimbabwe and the revolution, they dare not touch him because it would bring even more negative international publicity on Rhodesia.

Chamu: That is what I am saying, my brother! Listen, listen Andrew, when we become famous from our songs, the government won't touch us because the whole world will know about it!

Andrew (jokingly): Uhmm I like that, so maybe we could just sing a song about Smith, get arrested, go to jail, and sing some more from there and become famous quicker.

Muchazo (concerned): Guys if it is like that, I quit the band. I want to go to London. I do not want to go to jail.

Chamu (laughing): We are just playing.

Chamu is cut short by the arrival of Mr. Chaitezvi, agemate and friend of Majasi who walks with the aid of a cane. Chaitezvi is obviously agitated. He walks up to the veranda. Chamu stands and gives him his seat. Chamu joins Andrew sitting on the floor of the veranda looking towards the seated old men.

Majasi: Unedhoro come, come take a seat.

Chaitezvi drops his body onto the chair and takes a deep sigh.

Chaitezvi: Mupamombe I am at the end of my rope. Our village life was far better than this. At least there we had neighbours to turn to

Majasi: What is it?

Chaitezvi (turns to Andrew): Andrew, my son, get me a cup of water.

Andrew gets up and takes advantage of the pause to introduce his friends to his father's friend before dashing into the house to get the cup of water.

Andrew: Good afternoon sekuru. These are my friends Chamu and Muchazo.
Chamu and Muchazo greet the old man, who is obviously preoccupied.

Majasi (*speaking to Chaitezvi*): Unedhoro, today I was going to stay in the house and lay down because I am not feeling well but I came to sit outside to wait for you because I was able to find the herbs you asked for.

Chaitezvi: Oh, thank you. But let me tell you why it took me all day to come here.

Chaitezvi pauses to catch his breath and receive the cup of water proffered by Andrew.

Chaitezvi: Mupamombe our life in the village was not like this, there is no help. My muzukuru, Magedjo, the boy who takes care of me at my son's house, is in the police cells, locked up.

Majasi: That child?

Chaitezvi: Yes, that child. That boy is 14 not yet 15 years old but he has a big body like his mother. They locked him up because he was playing outside without his stupa.

Chamu: A 14-year-old boy does not have to carry an identification paper, does he?

Andrew: I do not think so. I thought stupas were for 18 and up.

Chaitezvi: My grandson is locked up. He has a mouth like his mother too. I do not know what he said to the police who arrested him.

Chamu: Was it police or soldiers on patrol?

Chaitezvi: I do not know.

Majasi: Where is he locked up?

Chaitezvi: Stodart Hall Police Station.

Majasi: Have you been there?

Chaitezvi: Have I been there? I was there last night. I went there early this morning and spent the day waiting for the member in charge.

Majasi: I know you told me his mother went to Fort Vic to her village with the girls but what about your son, his father?

Chaitezvi: You know he drives those big delivery trucks for Swift Transport?

Majasi: Yes

Chaitezvi: Well, they are busy these days with white people taking the gap, fleeing from Rhodesia to South Africa. So, he drove a truck to South Africa day before yesterday to transport household goods for a white, family moving to Johannesburg.

Andrew: Sekuru, what is the problem? He is a child they should not have arrested him for that.

Chaitezvi: The problem is I cannot find his birth certificate to take to Stodart Hall Police station to prove that he is just 14 or 15 whatever his age is.

Chamu: But surely the neighbours can tell the police he is just a big boy.

Chaitezvi: That's the problem. I wish we were in the country at our reservation. Everyone helps everyone. Here in Beatrice Cottages, they do not even greet me when they see me. They just look at me like I am a ghost.

Chamu: But there are neighbors there, right?

Chaitezvi: Yes, they are there. As I said, the boy's mother, my daughter-in-law, has a mouth on her. I am sure she has been insulting the neighbours, maybe that is why they do not care about what has happened in my son's house.

Muchazo: Hey Chamu, maybe we can go and talk to some of the neighbours and take one of them to Stodart Police station as a witness.

Muchazo turns to Chaitezvi to help assure him that they can help him.

Muchazo: Sekuru we are all from here, we were born here. Harare is our home. We know some of the friendly policemen at Stodart Police Station.

Andrew (*chimes in to assure Chaitezvi*): Yes sekuru, Chamu and Muchazo are ma-born-location (*children born in the African townships*) unlike people like me born in the reservations in the bundu.

The three young people laugh together at Andrew's self-deprecation humour.

Chaitezvi: Uhmm I would thank you from the bottom of my heart. That would bring my bp down my children.

Majasi: Talking about your bp and your sugar diabetes, what did you eat today?

Chaitezvi: Today? How about yesterday, last night? Nothing.

Majasi: That's not good. Magedjo's father did not leave money or food for you in the house?

Chaitezvi: That is not the problem. I am telling you. We have no neighbours to help. Living in this city is punishment on our generation from the ancestors, I tell you. There is food but Magedjo is the one who has been cooking for me and now he is locked up in the cells at Stodart Hall so there is nothing to eat.

Majasi: Nothing?

Chaitezvi: Just now when I came back from Stodart Hall, I put the kettle on the electric stove to boil water thinking at least I can make myself a cup of tea.

Majasi: So, you had tea?

Chaitezvi: No. The water won't boil.

Majasi: Why?

Chaitezvi: How would I know. I put water in the kettle on one of the plates on the stove as I have seen my grandson do. And so I put the thing with the electric wire in the thing and I sat down and waited for the water to boil.

Andrew: Sekuru you said you put the kettle with water on the stove, then you put the plug in the socket on the wall?

Chaitezvi: Yes. I did exactly that but even now as we sit here, I can tell you, the water in the kettle is as cold as it was when I put it on the stove.

Andrew: Did you turn the switch on?

Chaitezvi: What is that?

Andrew: The little flip thing that's on the socket where you plugged in the thing with the electric wire?

Chaitezvi: Uhmm who would know anything about that?

They all fall out laughing.

Chamu: Sekuru you just can't sit and look at the kettle on the stove and expect it to heat up unless you turn on the electricity.

They all continue to laugh.

Muchazo: Sekuru it is ok. When we go to your home with you to see about your muzukuru I can cook something for you while I wait for these guys to go sort out the problem with your muzukuru at Stodart.

Chaitezvi is touched. He breathes a sigh of relief.

Chaitezvi: Oh, my mother you a blessing, you, my children. Sure? You will come over and rescue me?

Andrew: It is not a problem we cannot let you starve when you have food in the house.

Andrew turns to his father.

Andrew: Mupamombe, you heard what is happening with your sawhira (friend). For me if I am on the road after six I am sure to run into the soldiers on patrol, I don't want to end up conscripted to call up. So let us leave you now.

Majasi: It is all very well my son. I am tired as it is I am turning in. I almost forgot.

Majasi hands Chaitezvi a small package wrapped in a newspaper.

Majasi: Oh here. My muzukuru John and I walked to the bushes beyond the houses and lucky for you we found the herb that will help you with your gout.

Chaitezvi: Oh Mupamombe, the ancestors sent you into my life. Thank you.

Majasi: Say no more go with these children. Andrew, call John tell him to come now before you go.

Muchazo: Rest is good baba. Stay well.

Majasi takes his friend's hand to get his attention.

Majasi: You Chaitezvi, just because my muroora is going to help cook for you doesn't mean you can start making plans for her with one of your many shiftless sons. She is spoken for. She is my muroora.

Everyone laughs.

Chaitezvi: Hahahaha I must admit the thought did cross my mind. Hahaha, you Mupamombes have all the luck with the ladies.

Majasi: I keep telling my son that. Now he has heard it for himself.

The two old men have a good hearty laugh.

Majasi: My children, I am glad Andrew has introduced us and I am especially glad that you are playing mbira together. Mbira is a sacred instrument it ushers in the spirits of our ancestors into our lives which is good because they watch over us. Please come and see me again. You can stop by anytime. I hope you will play your new songs for me to enjoy in the house.

Chamu: It was an honour to meet you Mupamombe. We shall do so.

Chamu turns to old Chaitezvi.

Chamu: Sekuru Unendoro (*referring to Chaitezvi*) let us get going.

(*Lights out*)

Scene 2

(Lights Up)

When the lights fade in, there is no one on the stage except a tall screen wide enough to cover the whole stage. The screen is painted like a cityscape of parks and office buildings dominated by a building with a sign that reads. "City of Salisbury Municipality, Revenue Department."

(Spotlight on the building on the Municipality, Revenue Dept, Bldg.)

The audience hears a phone ring. It is answered by an operator/receptionist.

Operator: Good afternoon, Revenue Department, how can I help you?

Voice: Good afternoon, may you please put me through to Mr. Choto's office.

Operator: Certainly madam. Who shall I say is calling.

Voice: It is his wife.

Operator: Hello Matron Choto, I did not recognize your voice.

Sally's Voice: Hello Anna, yes, it's me, can I speak to my husband.

Operator: Most certainly Matron, I will put him on the phone for you.

Sally's voice: Thank you Anna.

Operator: My pleasure Matron. (Pause) I have Mr. Choto on the line. Go ahead.

Rwizi: Hello Sally. I thought you would be on your way home by now.

Sally: We are going but Belinda is taking her time, she does have her family car, so there is no problem. We will be leaving soon. But darling, I have some really good news and I wanted to tell you about it and discuss it out here instead of at the house.

Rwizi does not respond.

Sally: You are not even curious about the good news?

Rwizi: Sorry I was a bit distracted. Give me a second so I can get rid of this paper, it needs my signature before we close shop for the day.

Sally: I can talk, and you can listen while you are doing your work, I know half the time you never listen to what I say anyway.

Rwizi: I can hear you, go ahead.

Sally: We were in the paper today.

Rwizi: What paper?

Sally: The Herald of course, you silly goose. (*she laughs*)

Rwizi: Honey, who is we?

Sally: Our club. The Salisbury African Ballroom Dancing Club.

Rwizi: Oh, but the club is always posting things in the announcements, the classified, or the society page.

Sally: But today was special, they posted the names of the regional finalists and of course You and I (Rwizi and Sally) were mentioned by name in the Herald because we are one of the finalist couples.

Rwizi: Uhmm that's nice. I like that.

101

Sally: I knew you would, I am bringing the paper home so you can see it.

Rwizi: I have today's Herald here in the office, I've just been busy...

Sally: Rwizi I know you, you just read the political headlines and business section, you never read the social announcements that's why you got me. It's my job to be your social secretary.

(*Light laughter again*)

Rwizi (*chuckles*): Ok, ok

Sally (*coquettishly*): And I did something else you are going to love me for.

Rwizi: What's that?

Sally: I know how you have been searching for a place for your father and you said you could not find any. Well, well, I got busy working on it myself. It turns out that Mary Katatu is now a Matron like me in Plumtree. Mary and I went to nursing school together and she is a very, very dear friend of mine even though she is not in Salisbury, that's why you do not hear me talk about her. Anyway, it so happens I called her in Plumtree to see if she had any idea where I should look. I told her that we needed a good home for your father a place that was clean and caring with good medical facilities. I told her the cost was not a problem.

Rwizi is quietly listening.

Sally: Rwizi, darling, are you listening?

Rwizi: Yes, I am here.

Sally: Well, you know the idea for a home for the aged is new for Africans in this country. I did not know anything about it myself until that time when I went on that tour of the UK sponsored by the British Council. That is where I learned that civilized people like the Europeans put their old people in homes where old people can be together with other old people. Over there in the UK they have some of the nicest places to put their old people in. Here it's a burden on us, which is sort of a primitive way of doing things, but that's typical African way of thinking. Anyway, you are right there are no places. You won't be able to find a place for your father around here because of the war. We now have people who fled the villages even sleeping on the pavements in front of shops. It's such a pity.

Rwizi: That is what I have been saying, right? There are no places for my father around here.

Sally: So, I spoke to Mary and guess what? Her hospital where she is the matron in charge does have a facility for old people. Like everywhere else, the place is full but Mary is my friend. She agreed to make a bed available for your father. She said its clean, its quiet and the great thing is, Mary, herself and her nursing staff, oversee the medical needs of he old people in the home. Now isn't that wonderful? I know you are going to thank me for this.

Rwizi: Sally, Plumtree is 300 miles away. That's more than a 6-hour drive from here.

Sally: Darling our car is one of the best cars on the road in Rhodesia today. Our Datsun 120Y can zip you right into Plumtree like a jet areophane. You love driving, that's why we bought the Datsun, remember?

Rwizi: Honey its too far. My father is a sickly old man.

Sally: All the more reason why he should be in a place where there is medical staff on call 24/7.

Silence.

A voice on Sally's end shouts: Sally, Matron Choto your chariot is waiting to take you to your palace. (Laughter).

Sally: Rwizi are you there?

Rwizi: Yes, I am here. *(Big sigh).*

Sally: Mary is doing us a big, big favour. I have to tell her one way or the other. I thought you would be grateful and as excited as I am, that we have found your father a decent place to live. Anyway, ballroom dancing competition finals are in 3 weeks. I must get the house in shape which I cannot do as long as the issue of your father is not resolved. So, you better get moving on other plans, if you don't want my friend's help. Bye, darling, see you at home.

Rwizi: Ok, see you. Bye.

Click. The phone line goes dead.

CURTAIN

HIGH CLASS NATIVES
Ballroom Dancers & Mbira Players

ACT Four

Early evening Choto's house.

The curtain opens in Choto house family living/dining room. On the record player is a song by Elvis Pressley, "Love Me Tender".
Rwizi and Sally are sitting together, drinking cocktails. John is on the floor in front of his grandfather with crayons in his hands, drawing on art paper.

Sally looks at her watch and stands and goes to open the door.

>Sally: Belinda should be coming any minute now, let's get some fresh air into the house.
>
>Rwizi: Is Sam coming too?
>
>Sally: I don't know, but he is dropping her off.
>
>John: Yeah, yeah Auntie Bee is coming. She always brings me sweets.
>
>Sally: Ok John, I do not mind her giving you sweets, but I do not want you asking anyone for sweets.
>
>John: Yes mother.

There is a sound of a car pulling up by the road in front of the house. We hear voices coming from the car. Then at the door appears Belinda, Sally's friend. She is an attractive well-dressed woman about the same age as Sally, behind her is SAM, Belinda's husband. He is a tall equally handsome man who is in a hurry.

>Sally: Right on time Bee.
>
>Belinda: I am always on time unlike some people I know.
>
>Sally: That's what I like about you, you keep time like white people.

Belinda: Do not start with me with your "white people are great nonsense."

They share a laugh as Belinda puts down her handbag and finds a seat.
Sam steps into the house behind his wife and sits beside her.
They put their hands together and respectfully clap their hands as Belinda greets Rwizi's father, Majasi.

Belinda: Sekuru Mupamombe, makadiyiko? Tavanenguva tisati taonana. (*Sekuru how are you? We have not seen you in a while*).

Majasi returns the greeting, clapping his own hands.

Majasi: Ndiripo zvangu, kananeni ndafara kuku onayi. (I am well, happy to see you too).

Belinda: John, aren't you happy to see your Auntie Bee and Uncle Sam.

John: I am happy to see you Auntie Bee. Do you want to see what I drew for sekuru?

Belinda: Of course, I want to see the drawings of my favorite nephew.

Sam: I just popped in to say hello. I will be back I have to dash to the store.

Sally *(jokingly)*: All good, we do not need you away. We just want Belinda.

Everyone laughs as Sam gets up to leave.

Sam *(in good humour laughing)*: Well, here she is. I must run. Rwizi I will see you, save some of that scotch for me.

Sam leaves.

Rwizi : I will be waiting for him. I have some scotch to drink with that man.

Belinda: I am sure he will need it. The store is not doing good.

Rwizi: Really? What's going on?

Belinda: It is Saturday, the shop is supposed to be busy, so he has gone there out of habit to help but it's not really necessary. You will see him after he closes. He will tell you.

Rwizi: So, it's that bad?

Belinda: Right now, business is practically dead. People have no money. People are losing their jobs with the war and the sanctions. But hey, give me the drink I came for.

Rwizi mixes her drink.

Rwizi: Gin and tonic, the usual right?

Belinda: Of course...

Sally: Bee you should try the vodka and cranberry juice. It's delicious.

Berlinda (laughing): Only after the gin has killed my taste buds, then I can drink anything.

The Elvis Presley music continues to play on the stereo system.

Belinda: Sally pleaseee. Give us some soul music from Rwizi's collection, I know he has - Otis Redding, or Wilson Pickett or Percy Sledge.

Sally: Elvis is king of rock and roll; you know I love Elvis.

Belinda: Poor Rwizi, she makes you listen to Elvis Presley all day.

Rwizi *(laughing)*: It's a sickness my wife has.

Sally *(laughing)*: Rwizi you know you love Elvis.

Belinda: Cause you make him.

As Belinda is talking, she is reaching into her handbag and finds what she is looking for.

Belinda: Here John, here is a treat for you and something for sekuru. His favorite biscuits, Eat One Now.

John: Thank you, thank you Auntie Bee. I knew you would bring me sweets.

Belinda: And here is something else for sekuru. *(Belinda gives John a hat.)* Give sekuru his new hat too.

Majasi: Uhmm my ancestors. I don't believe this. I was not expecting this Auntie Bee.

Majasi claps his hands in appreciation.

Majasi: Ah thank you, masibanda *(her totem)* I like Eat One Now biscuits. I will wear the hat when I go outside, it's been hot lately. Thank you so much. I needed this hat. But I will eat the biscuits tomorrow, I think my stomach is upset.

Belinda: Ah sekuru, you sound a little wheezy too? What's going on?

Majasi: I am just tired. I will be alright after I lie down.

John: Sekuru did not play with me today, he was tired.

Majasi: I will be alright soon. Us, old people, we just need a little rest, that's all.

Belinda: Sally doesn't sekuru seem sick to you? Did you take his temperature.

Sally: I am sure he will be ok. He is just tired as he said.

Belinda: Do you have a thermometer in the house?

Sally: No, John stepped on it and broke it last time I used it on him.

Belinda puts her drink down and walks to Majasi.

Belinda: Sekuru let me feel your temperature?

Majasi: Please do, when a senior nurse like you talks, I must listen.

Belinda puts her fingers on Majasi's head to feel his temperature.

Belinda: You are a little warm, I was afraid you may have a fever or something, there is a bug spreading around these days you know.

Rwizi: So you think he may have some kind of flu bug.

Belinda: I do not know. Sekuru, how is your bowel movement?

Majasi: Not good. I may be constipated.

Belinda: Sally, I do not know, what do you think? I think a good dose of milk of magnesia may help sekuru.

Sally: Uhmm we do not have any in the house.

Rwizi: Though it's Sunday tomorrow, the pharmacy will be open. I will get him some.

Belinda: Sekuru when you get the milk of magnesia, take a double dose and eat some vegetables that will help you become regular.

John: Sekuru can eat my vegetables. I do not want them.

They all laugh.

Belinda: No John you eat your own vegetables otherwise you be sick like sekuru.

Sally: John listen to Auntie Bee otherwise no more sweets.

John: Yes mother.

Belinda returns to her seat.

Majasi: Thank you Auntie Bee. I think I will go and lay down now.

Belinda: You will be okay sekuru, just take the medicine and be sure to go out for a walk and get some fresh air during the day.

John: I walk with sekuru.

Belinda: Good boy. That's why Auntie Bee likes you John, you take care of sekuru.

John: Sekuru is my best friend.

Belinda: Really? Just for that you will get more sweets next time I come.

Rwizi stands up.

Rwizi: Baba, do you need help getting up.

Majasi: No, no I am fine.

Rwizi: John let's go see about sekuru's bed.

Rwizi, John and Majasi leave the room.

Belinda: Sally it's a great thing you and Rwizi are doing, taking care of sekuru. He is really a special guy. A gentle soul.

Sally (*nonchalantly*): Oh, we take very good care of him.

Belinda: And it's good for John to have his grandfather around in the house. How I wish my father or Sam's father lived in our house like you have sekuru here. My two boys would have someone else to relate to like we did in the village. Grandparents are more accessible than your own father and mother.

Sally: I wouldn't know, I never had any.

Belinda: I did and I am better for it. Believe me even though you may not see it now, little John is going to be a better man because of his sekuru being around him.
Sally: I wouldn't worry about John's future like that; we send him to best European school in Rhodesia. They will teach him to be a better man.

Belinda: There you go again with your European obsession. Your child needs African culture to know about "hunhu", "ubuntu".

Sally: Europeans can teach him that.

Belinda: Europeans cannot teach your child anything except to be a European.

Sally: My point exactly. My son is going to be a European.
Belinda: I give up. You are hopeless. Let me get myself another drink.

Rwizi returns to the room.

Rwizi (*chuckling*): Thank you Bee. My father looks like he is feeling better already.

Belinda: Old people need watching over because sometimes they forget to do simple things like drinking water. Which is very important.

Sally jumps into the conversation.

Sally: Bee did I tell you we were in the Herald?

Belinda *(laughing):* How many times are you going to tell me Sally?

Sally: You are laughing now, you won't be laughing when Rwizi and I are crowned the king and queen of the Rhodesia Classical Ballroom Dancing Champions.

Belinda (laughing): Uhmm you can keep your ballroom dancing, some of us are not high-class natives like you.

113

Rwizi joins Belinda, laughing.

Sally: You can laugh all you want. We, the high-class-natives, as you call us, are in the newspapers and you are not.

Belinda: Who cares to be in the newspaper?

Sally: I do. It's prestige. People know who I am.

Belinda: Sally, sometimes I think you do not have it all upstairs.
Belinda turns to Rwizi.

Belinda: Rwizi please put some wicked Wilson Pickett on. I feel like dancing.

Sally: Why don't we put Beethoven's waltz music on so we can practice.

Belinda and Rwizi (*together*): No, no, no ballroom music please.

Sally: You two are barbarians, you have no culture.

Belinda: Go away with that barbarian stuff, I dragged Sam to join the ballroom dancing club with me because of you, but I am African. We love soul music!

Sally: Rwizi do you know what this ignorant African woman is calling us because we are sophisticated?

Rwizi: What?

Sally: High class natives, that's what she calls us.

Rwizi laughs:

CURTAIN

HIGH CLASS NATIVES
Ballroom Dancers & Mbira Players

ACT Five

MBIRA MUSIC IS PLAYING.

Same early evening Mlambo's house.

When the curtain opens, we are in the same setting, Beatrice Cottages neighbourhood at Mlambo's house, which is like Choto's residence. As before, the house is sparsely furnished. The scene opens in the same living room. There are sofas along the wall, a coffee table and a stereo system in one of the corners. There are drums, guitars, mbiras and microphones on stands scattered about. Chamu and Muchazo are in the middle of playing a sad traditional mbira song. Andrew knocks and enters the room. They nod to him to join the song. Andrew picks up a mbira instrument and joins them. As before Andrew ends up being the lead mbira player in the songs they play. Finally, they stop playing.

Andrew: Guys playing mbiras with you is great but walking from Matapi Hostels to Beatrice Cottages is no joke. I need time to rest.

Muchazo: Andrew, we have 2 hours before the meeting starts and the bhira is much later, so relax. You can even take a nap on one of these sofas.

Chamu: Well, my brother, from what I hear from Muchazo, your accommodation troubles may be over.

Andrew: Really?

Muchazo: Maybe.

Andrew: Maybe what? Please tell me.

Muchazo: Maybe you will like it, maybe you won't.

Andrew: Muchazo, I am at the point where anything is better than what I got now, because honestly, right now I have nothing.

Muchazo: Do not say that. You got me.

Andrew: Oh, sorry I didn't mean it like that. But you know what I mean. I am at the end of my rope.

Muchazo: Here is what we got. My uncle, who owns the Tayenda Bus Line, has a 14-year-old son who was in boarding school at Derera Mission, in Nhowe. You know the school?

Andrew: Of course, I know the school is not too far from my old school.

Muchazo: The school is closed. There have been too many deadly battles fought in and around that area between the boys and the Rhodesia Army, the school administrators fear that it's just a matter of time before they become hostages of either side.

Andrew: Where are you going with this?

Muchazo: Patience my dear.

Chamu (*mimicking Muchazo*): Patience my dear.

Andrew: Ok my name is patience.

They all laugh.

Muchazo: Anyway, my uncle's son was attending that school.

Andrew: What grade was he?

Muchazo: Form 2. And he was supposed to finish Form 2 there this year and go to Goromonzi or St Ignatius Secondary school for Form 3 next year.

Andrew: It does not matter how much money you have; those are not easy schools to get into.

Muchazo: Which brings us to the issue of your accommodation.

Andrew: Really? How?

Muchazo: My uncle stopped by our house the day before yesterday. I heard him talking to my mother, his sister, telling her about the situation with Ambrose, his son. He does not know what to do.

Chamu: The uncle has done well with his many businesses, but he barely finished primary school.

Muchazo: My uncle is smart that's why he is such a successful businessman, but academics is not his thing.

Andrew: I am still not getting that part about my accommodation solution.

Muchazo: My uncle is determined to have his son continue with his Form 2 education. He wants Ambrose to sit and take his Form 2 examinations in November even though his school is closed. By the way, I know the boy, Ambrose. He is just as smart as his father. Without this interruption caused by the war, I am sure he would pass Form 2 with flying colours.

Andrew: Ok, go on.

Muchazo: My uncle trusts me. He thinks I am a good girl and a good influence on Ambrose.

Chamu *(chuckling)*: That's debatable but who is debating anything nowadays of war.

Muchazo: Get away Chamu. I am a good girl.

Andrew: And a smart one too.

Muchazo: Fact.

Andrew: Chamu, please stop interrupting!

Chamu: Ok. Ok.

Muchazo: Anyway, I suggested that Ambrose continue his education with an in-house private tutor. I also told him I knew a guy I trust who had finished and passed Form 4 with exceptional marks in Maths and Science.

Andrew (hunching his shoulders with a smile on his face): That would be Mr. Andrew Choto, if I was not mistaken.

Chamu: You are not mistaken, good buddy. Muchazo asked me about it before she pitched the idea to her uncle, and I told her it was a brilliant idea. Kill two birds with one stone.

Andrew (*laughing*): I am not a bird, and I am not about to allow anyone to kill me.

Muchazo: Chamu is colourful with his language as usual. But true, we discussed it, and he encouraged me to do it.

Andrew: Thanks guy! So, what did your uncle say?

Muchazo: He wants to meet you. But there's only one problem. Even though the servants' quarters are vacant, they are reserved for his garden boy. So, he is also looking for someone to tend his flowers and the lawn. You can get the

119

tutoring job, but you can't have the accommodation because it's for his live-in gardener.

Andrew: I don't care. I can be a garden boy. I grew up taking care of plants. A flower and a lawn are nothing but grass to me. I will be a garden boy. I don't care.

Muchazo: Really? Ok so if you are not busy, (*sarcastically*) tomorrow, but if your calendar is full, you can always accommodate him with a meeting two weeks from now._(*She laughs*).

Andrew: Police or no police, soldiers or no soldiers on the road tonight I will go and meet him anywhere. Where does he live?

Chamu: Marimba Park.

Andrew: Marimba Park? That's where the rich, rich Africans live. I hear they have more money there than here in Beatrice Cottages, of course my sister-in-law, Sally, would not agree with that statement.

Chamu: You are correct buddy. I have been to Marimba Park, but you have to see it for yourself.

Muchazo: If he likes you, you can move in anytime. I think. The servant's quarters have 2 bedrooms and a kitchen.

Andrew: I want my father to live with me. I want the servant's quarters. That would be great.

Muchazo: Very well it is settled. I will call him tomorrow and set up your meeting.

Andrew grabs Muchazo and hugs her.

Chamu: Hey, hey enough of the love stuff. Now let's deal with our problem.

Andrew: What problem?

Chamu: You, me and Muchazo is the only band we got.

Andrew: What happened to Maxwell, Ticha, Tinotenda and Zodwa, I thought everything was going well. That's why I signed up to be in the band.

Chamu: They are gone.

Andrew: You mean like gone, gone? Like they skipped the border to Mozambique?

Chamu: Yes, my brother.

Andrew: Woaw. But I am not mad at them. If I could, I would too. This Rhodesia Ian Smith bullshit must end. It's our generation that must do something about ending it. If our generation doesn't do it, then who? Our elders are too old for it.

Chamu: Franz Fanon said, every generation must find its purpose, and fulfil it or betray it. We are at that point, my brother. I know my purpose. I have decided not to cross the border. I am not going to Zambia or Mozambique to join Zanla or Zipra. Something tells me that Zi-Mbira band is my role in this fight with white people to the death. My mbira music, as ordinary as it is, serves a purpose. The struggle for Zimbabwe is mbira music. It will lead our people to victory. Mbira music reminds the spirits of our ancestors not to forget us, it calls them to come down and lead us to victory as Mbuya Nehanda did. I want to be a lawyer. I want to stand in court and defend my people. I know somehow that's going to happen if we continue to play our mbira music. If I cannot be a lawyer in Rhodesia, I will be a lawyer in Zimbabwe. Mark my words.

Andrew: I am with you Chamu on that. We were given the gift to play mbira as we do, for a purpose. But tell me this, boys and girls who leave to go join the freedom fighters do not broadcast the fact. So how do you know that they actually skipped the border?

Muchazo (misty eyed): Zodwa and I are like sisters. She knew I would be worried, so she left me a small, small note telling me not to worry. But I am worried, they could be in Botswana now or in Zambia or Mozambique. Nobody knows. For all I know they could be in some cell being tortured by Rhodesia solders right now. (*She is crying*).

Andrew: I am sure wherever they are, they are safe because I have never heard of anyone being arrested for thinking what they are thinking. They are not walking around with signs on their foreheads saying we are going to Mozambique to come back and be terrorists.

Chamu: Andrew our band's troubles are not just that.

Chamu turns to Muchazo.

Chamu: Muchazo you might as well tell him the rest.

Muchazo reaches in her pocket and hands Andrew a letter.
Andrew looks at the letter and exclaims.

Andrew: It's from the British Council.

Andrew reads the letter in silence while Chamu and Muchazo look at him.
Andrew finishes reading the letter and gives it back to Muchazo.

Andrew: Woaw, you got your scholarship to go to England to study nursing.

Chamu: Isn't that exciting? The scholarship pays for airfare, tuition and room and board.

Muchazo: I am not leaving just yet. I still must apply for a passport which the government may deny me.

Muchazo takes Andrew into her arms.

Muchazo: Are you ok?

Andrew: Yes, yes, I am ok. But it's just that when I thought my luck was beginning to change everything is not what it was, nothing is there.

Muchazo: I am nothing?

Andrew: Of course, you are everything to me.

Muchazo: So why the long face?

Andrew: I was excited because I thought we were all going to be together in the Zi-Mbira Band, but all the band members are gone. I thought I had you, but you are off to England.

Muchazo: But Andrew, I thought the most important thing for you was to get a job and to be able to have your father live with you?

Andrew: Yet…but

Muchazo: But what? I fixed it for you. My uncle is going to give you the job and it will be up to you to take a bedroom in his house or the 2 bedroom servant's quarters in the back. You will be earning a salary.

Andrew: But you will not be here?

Muchazo: Don't you know that there is a thing called airmail? We will write to each other.

Chamu: Andrew my brother. Mbira music does not require a zillion people to be in the band. Do not sweat it. This music belongs to the ancestors. They will give us new band members. Band members our ancestors chose not ones we choose. Let your girlfriend go to England in love with you. I have known Muchazo since she was a little girl on our street. She is a serious person. Be happy for her and for yourself. I am telling you; this is going to work out well for both of you.

Andrew and Muchazo hug again.

CURTAIN

HIGH CLASS NATIVES
Ballroom Dancers & Mbira Players

ACT Six

Scene 1

Choto's House - A few days later – night

When the curtain opens. Beethoven's Waltz in E-Flat Major is playing.

Rwizi and Sally are in their living room dancing to a waltz followed by a foxtrot classical music record. They are dressed in ballroom dancing costumes, a gown for Sally and tails for Rwizi.

> Sally: Honey change the record. Let's practice the foxtrot again. We keep stepping on each other's feet on the left turn.

> Rwizi: Sally, I am tired. We have been practicing for more than an hour since my father and John went to bed.

> Sally: I like it when we are dressed up for rehearsal, it feels like the real thing.

> Rwizi: But I'm tired. I worked the whole day; I didn't know I was coming home to this ordeal.

> Sally: Oww com'on darling, this is not an ordeal. I know you love ballroom dancing as much as I do, and you are going to thank me for this 'ordeal' as you call it when we are crowned king and queen of the competition. Practice makes perfect.

> Rwizi: Practice makes tired! Ok, at least let me get myself a drink.

> Sally: Make me one too. I am going to the bathroom. I will be right back.

Rwizi is mixing drinks when there is a knock at the door.
Rwizi goes to the door and finds an old woman standing at the door.

Rwizi: Manheru. Tigakubatsireyi neyi? *(Good evening how can I help you?)*

Old Woman: Manheru. Ndipohere panogara nurse anobva kwaMutoko? *(Good evening. Is this the house where the nurse from Mutoko lives?)*

Rwizi: Hongu. *(Yes)*

Old woman: Ini ndiri amai guru vake. Ndauya kuzomuona. *(I am her aunt; I have come to visit her.)*

Rwizi: Pindayi zvenyu. *(Please come in.)*

The old woman comes in and sits on the floor beside the door. She has a bundle of clothes by her side.

Sally returns to the room from her bathroom visit. She stiffens when she notices the woman sitting on the floor.

Old woman (*in Shona*): Manheru. *(Good evening).*

Sally *(in English)*: Good evening.

Sally turns around and calls Rwizi to come to the bedroom.

(The lights dim out)

(Lights up in the bedroom)

Sally: That woman in the living room, she is one of your numerous relatives?

Rwizi: No.

Sally: That's funny, Arimando has never done this before. When we took him on, I told him no relatives here. It's a pity but I am going to have to fire him. Rules are rules. He is forgetting his place.

Rwizi: That woman didn't come here for Arimando. She came here for you.

Sally: Me? What would she want with me?

Rwizi: She says she is a relative of yours.

Sally laughs.

Sally: Me? A relative? You must be joking.

She laughs again.

The lights follow them into the living room and they both sit down.

Sally: My husband tells me that you're here for me. I don't believe we have ever met.

The old woman tucks the fringes of her skirt under her legs. She is clearly uncomfortable.

Sally: Have we?

Old woman (*in Shona*): Uhm, uhm. I have come a long way, my daughter. Three months ago, we had a beer drink at our village in Dande. We were raising money for our next season's maize crop. As you know, the guerrillas, I mean the freedom fighters, live among us. They do not bother us but the Rhodesia Army soldiers; they are the trouble. They came to our beer drink and attacked but the guerrillas were ready for them. All the soldiers were killed on the spot. Next morning, the tiyo-tiyo bird (spotter plane) came followed by another. They bombed the whole village with fire and napalm. I don't know whether you know what napalm is, but it burns off the skin. Some of us died but others were lucky. We escaped to the mission school. The kind headmaster there put us in the school truck today and helped us come to Harare. We have been living in tents at the mission since.

Sally: I am very sorry to hear that but you didn't answer my question. You told my husband that we are related?

Old woman (*in Shona*): Yes. So, when I got the chance to leave the tents I came to Harare. We arrived as the sun was setting.

Sally: You have said you are related to me; I don't have any relatives. Not African relatives anyway.

Old Woman: Aren't you the daughter of Verenika, the daughter of Samusoni, whose totem is Shumba?

Sally: Who are you?

Old woman (*in Shona*): A long time ago, in the fourth year of drought, after the termites, you were born, there was no food in the land those days and we only had hand-outs from the government, your mother and I were sisters, I am your mother's older sister, I am your aunt Sophia.

Sally: And what is my name?

Old woman (*in Shona*): I never heard anyone refer to you by name, but the old woman who worked for Doctor Cederic told me where you lived.

Sally: You do not even know my name. Yet you say you are my mother's older sister. And you have the gall to come into my house and sit there and tell me I am your niece? Where were you when I didn't have any relatives? Where was I born? Why don't you mention that since you are so well informed about me? Go on, tell us where was I born? Where did I grow up?

Old woman: I don't know.

Sally: Oh yes you know. The truth of my miserable life story will not bother my husband, he knows all about it. Tell us that you know that I was born under a bush in the forest like a wild animal. Go on tell me all about that. Tell me about how you all drove my mother into the darkness of the night to live like a wild animal and sacrificed a cow to appease some demon spirit to take all your troubles and load them on my mother, to bring you good fortune and rain. Tell us about how all your rituals and roots were thrown on my mother's head. If you brought any of that thrash into my house, let me tell you that it does not work.

Sally stands.

Sally (*in Shona*): Out! Out! Get out of my house, you witch! Relative? Me? Do you know where I grew up? The only relative I have is a white missionary. Do you hear me? I grew up in a dormitory? Where were you KAFFIRS when I was born? Relative? Get out!

Rwizi: Take it easy honey.

Sally: Stay out of this.

Old Woman: I came with the hope that you would give an old woman, your aunt, a place to flee the war. I am your mother's sister. People make mistakes.

130

Sally: Woman, my patience is very, very thin, I said get out of my house.

Old Woman (*in Shona crying*): What could I do? My husband would have never accepted another mouth to feed. You were born in the days of hunger. Nobody knew who your father was. Your mother tried to hang herself on the msasa tree three times before you were born and she never told me or anyone else in the village why,

Sally (*in Shona*): As if you didn't know, your father was my father. Now get out of my house.

Old Woman (*in Shona*): Spirits of the dead. What? Father? To do that?

Sally (*in Shona*): You pretend as if you didn't know, you knew, just as everyone else in your family knew. I was part of your ritual, isn't that why my mother and I had to live in the forest far away from other people, uh?

Old Woman (*in Shona*): I swear on my mother's grave, I never knew this. How could I?

Sally (*in English*): I don't care, I don't know you. You do not exist. I said get out.

Old Woman (*in Shona*): I have travelled all this way to hide from the war. Our village is gone. I don't know anybody else in this big city. Where will I go?

Sally: I don't care, you should have made another sacrifice in your village to stop the war, or whatever, just get out, you filthy thing.

Old Woman: In the name of God, I beg you.
Sally goes to the kitchen. She returns with a broom in her hands.

Sally: I am going to kill you

Rwizi jumps from his seat and grabs the broom from her mid-air.

Rwizi: Sally, take it easy.
They struggle for possession of the broom. The old woman gets up.

Old Woman *(in Shona)*: No, no! I will leave, I will leave but I am your aunt. I will leave although I don't know where to go.

Sally: OUououououououttttttt! And take your filthy rugs with you, whatever roots and evil you brought into my house will not work!!

Rwizi: It's alright, I will drive her to Musika, to the buses.

Sally: Not in my car, you won't. She will go like she came on her bare feet.

The old woman collects her bundle and backs out of the house into the darkness of the night, protesting.

Old Woman *(in Shona)*: I have no evil roots.

Sally *(in Shona)*: Yes, you do, I know you kaffirs.

She slams the door.
She stands motionless for a while and sighs deeply.

Rwizi: You didn't have to be so hard on the old woman.

Sally: What do you know about being hard on someone? Have you ever known fear of the darkness, spooks in the night? Did people run away from you when you were a child?

Rwizi: All the more reason why you should have been kind to that old woman. Your childhood should make you compassionate.

Sally: Compassionate my foot! That old witch and her family knew I was out there even when my mother was dying and they pretended we didn't exist. Do you realize that had it not been for Dr Cedrick, I would have frozen to death sitting with my mother's dead body?

Rwizi: I understand but she is just an old woman.

Sally: That woman claimed to be my aunt not yours, so stop grilling me.

Rwizi: Yes honey.

Sally: Which reminds me, do you know that your father is teaching John witchcraft?

Rwizi: Witchcraft?

Sally: Yes, witchcraft. He took John to the forest to dig some roots, claiming it was medicine.

Rwizi: But that's not witchcraft. Father is a competent herbalist.

Sally: I have been as patient as anyone can be. I have not interfered with your relationship with your relatives. I have even let you accommodate your brother in our house as if it was a restaurant. Your father has been here for almost a year

133

now, I have tried my best for you and what gratitude do I get? Your relatives teach my son to speak vernacular, your brother soils my house with his sweat, and your father is not only content to make my son a kaffir but a warlock on top of that. No Rwizi. I told you before and I have said it, time and time again, you must make a choice. I will not permit my house to be turned into a village, especially if I am going to live in it. I have given you time and that time is up.

Rwizi: I am trying

Sally: There is nothing to try but to do. I found a place for you in Plumtree, you'd better take it, so you have no excuse.

Rwizi: I am…

Sally: I am not going to argue with you, all I know is that our dance competition championship finals is three weeks away, if I were you, I would do the sensible thing now as later, because you will have to do this at some point.

CURTAIN

HIGH CLASS NATIVES
Ballroom Dancers & Mbira Players

ACT Seven

Rwizi's Office - Two weeks later – **afternoon**

Rwizi is in his office sitting behind a desk. The office is appropriately furnished for his position.
A porter knocks on the door and enters the office.

Porter: Excuse me sir, there is a young man at the reception who says he is your brother, he would like to see you.

Rwizi: Ha? Show him in.

The porter exits.
Enter Andrew.

Rwizi: Eh, Mupamombe, haven't seen you in a while.

Andrew: I've been looking for a job.

Rwizi: Yes. I know it's rough, so how have you been?

Andrew: As if you cared.

Rwizi: What do you mean - as if I cared? What are you trying to say?

Andrew: Nothing that you don't already know.

Rwizi: Look, I am busy. I don't have time for that kind of attitude. Say what you came to say, I have work to do.

Andrew: Where is the old man?

Rwizi: Oh father?

Andrew: Yes.

Rwizi: I don't think I ever told you this, but my wife and I have been having problems of our own. Nothing to do with you or baba. So, everything has been tense around the house. You know? Sally has a very difficult job - too much responsibility being a matron at Harare Hospital and I have all these problems myself in this office.

Andrew: Are you trying to explain something or are you just confirming what Arimando told me about my eating at your house?

Rwizi: What?

Andrew: Arimando did tell me that I couldn't eat there anymore according to your wife's instructions.

Rwizi: We didn't say that. Sally only said that you and John were soiling the house when you played in there and suggested that you eat on the veranda.

Andrew: And baba?

Rwizi: You don't understand. Sally never said anything about dad eating in the house.

Andrew: Anyway, not to worry, since that day, I haven't been to your house, and I would not have gone there today except to see my father.

Rwizi: So, what have you been living on? We didn't want you to take it like that.

Andrew: 'Brother' that's all water under the bridge now and it's not what I came here for. Arimando told me that you took dad home. Where is home? Our village was burnt to ground so I got confused. Where did you' take dad to?

137

Rwizi: That's what I have been trying to tell you. If we could have worked out something, some place for dad to stay until I sorted out something or until the end of the war, or if we had a relative here in Harare.

Andrew: What are you talking about? What relative does dad need? We are Africans, aren't we? I don't know about other cultures but in Africa, there is no relative more related to you than a father and a son, than a brother and a brother, from the same blood. This means, father, you and me. That's relatives.

Rwizi: But there is also my wife and child. If you had a job, you could have had a place for dad to stay.

Andrew: I do have a job, that's what I had gone to tell dad when I went to your precious house today.

Rwizi: A job? Congratulations. I knew you could do it. Boy I am very proud of you. We, Mupamombes, were born to success. While everyone is crying about the economy, the war and the scarcity of jobs, you just went out and got one. Where is your job?

Andrew: I work in Marimba Park, it's not much but it's a job.

Rwizi: Marimba Park? What would a person with your level of education do in Marimba Park? You are a personal secretary to some big shot, eh?

Andrew: It's a job where I can eat and dad can live with me in the boy's *kaya*.

Rwizi: No, you are an educated person, you must get yourself a nice place to rent in Highfields.

138

Andrew: Hey, hey hold it. I can't afford a nice place in Highfields. All I wanted was some food in my stomach and a place for my father. Fortunately for him and I, there are still some Africans who have more money than some people I could mention, and they still believe in African values. You see, my African boss does not mind my father or you yourself to come and live with me. He knows the war in the villages is a necessary evil and feels sorry for his own. So, where is dad, I want to take him to my boss.

Rwizi: Father is not here.

Andrew: I know that, Arimando told me remember?

Rwizi: You see, I didn't know you had found a job, so I took him to a place in Plumtree.

Andrew: Where? Plumtree? To do what in Plumtree?

Rwizi: As I said, I didn't know you had a job, so I took him to a place for old people.

Andrew: You what?

Rwizi: What could I do? I didn't know you had a job.

Andrew: That has nothing to do with anything. Rwizi you are man who is scared to drive to Mhondoro which is only fifty miles away from here and yet you would have the courage to face army roadblocks and possible ambushes to take your father to Plumtree and throw him into a place for old people'?

Andrew glares at Rwizi who remains silent.

Andrew: Do you know that that man is a sick man? How could you take your own father to a place like that? Which African do we know, you and I, whom we grew up with who has a father in place built for foreign blacks, people from Zaire or Malawi who have no children here? How could you abandon your father a thousand miles away from nowhere?

Rwizi: Plumtree is only 300 miles.

Andrew: 3 miles, 300 miles, 3000 miles what is the difference? How could you, you are the man whose life and education was paid for by everything that father and mother had. To throw that same father into a pit of strangers like he was an old dirty blanket? Did your wife put you to this?

Rwizi: It's just for a short while. I did it for him. There he will be with other old people his age.

Andrew (*almost shouting*): Baba? Old? Baba is as young as your son John is. Did you ever see them play together? Did you? Our father who could have been the chief of all the Mupamombes if the white man had not taken our chieftainship and given it to Tsombes. A man who owned seventy heard of cattle before the white man forced him to sell them to white farmers. A man who sacrificed and turned his back on everything to see that his son would be the first graduate in Mhondoro Reserve and the first to drive a car over Nyokandove River. And all that sacrifice for what, to live the life of a destitute African labourer from God knows where? You? To throw our father into a hut like an old useless farm labourer the white man is done with? How could you? Why? Our father is rich, he has a son who has this big office, a three bedroomed house, everything that others have had to go to war for. Eh?

Rwizi: I took him there myself, it's not that bad, anyway it's just for a short while.

140

Andrew shouts.

Andrew: You are damn right!

Rwizi: Lower your voice, you're going to attract attention.

Andrew (*shouts louder*): Dammmmn Right! I want them all to know the real Mr. Rwizi Choto whose father lives in a hole covered by plastic.

Rwizi: This is not going to help anybody.

Andrew: Where in Plumtree is he? I intend to go and get him now.

Rwizi: That's good. He is at Plumtree Shelter for the Old, ask anybody when you get there, they will direct you. Here is some money for the bus.

Andrew: If it had not been for the fact that I don't have any money of my own, I wouldn't touch this. This is the last time I will ever accept anything from you. We are no longer brothers, brother!

He slams the door and exits.

CURTAIN

HIGH CLASS NATIVES
Ballroom Dancers & Mbira Players

ACT Eight

Next Day – Afternoon

PLUMTREE: Andrew is sitting on a tree stump by a roadside. Two signposts stand behind him – one sign proclaims, 'Bus Stop' and the other is a lettered sign with a big directional arrow pointing with the words, 'Plumtree Shelter For The Old' 500 yards. Beside him is a paper bag containing some of Majasi's clothes and the hat that Belinda gave him. The conversation is in Shona.

Andrew is sobbing loudly.

Two men dressed in combat fatigues, with rifles hanging on their shoulders, approach Andrew, one of the men is carrying a package wrapped in brown paper bag.

    Man 1: Uhm, excuse me.

Andrew lifts his head and looks at the men, his eyes are flooded with tears.

    Man1: Excuse us, you are the comrade from Harare, aren't you?

    Andrew: Yes.

    Man 1: Matron Mary Katatu from the hospital told us about your father, please accept our condolences.

They take his hand in turn and shake it.

    Man 2: It's sad. We had not even had him here long.

    Man1: It was so sudden; I still don't understand it.

Andrew shakes his head.

    Man 2: We hear your home is in Mhondoro Reserve?

Andrew bursts into tears.

Andrew: Yes.

Man 1: Uh, so far away, it is sad for an old man to die so far away from home.

Man 2: Uh, it was so sudden, and the nurses said they thought that it was just the flu.

Man 1: That's the way of life comrade, no one ever knows when they go.

Andrew looks at the man.

Andrew: He didn't have to die here, like this. *(He points at the paper bag beside him)* To leave his clothes in a paper bag. My father did not deserve this.

Man 1: There is nothing to do comrade, these are days of hunger and hardship. Today, Africans have nothing in this country. All an African has and lives with are the clothes on his body and dies the same.

Andrew: You don't understand my father did not have to die *(he stammers)* to die this way.

Man 1: We hear you comrade, it's sad, uh, uh, have you made any arrangements for his burial.

Andrew: I don't know what to do. They sent the body to the mortuary, if I had not arrived when I did, I don't know what they would have done. I am going back to Salisbury to tell my brother about his death, I am sure he will be happy that he is dead.

Man 2: Happy?

Andrew: Yes, happy. My brother brought him here to die. He could have cared for him and given him the comfort our old people deserve. He killed my father. My brother has a big house and a big job. My brother is a rich man. And this is what he did for his father - death in a shelter like a useless pauper.

Andrew resumes his sobbing.

Man 2: Comrade you are a man, life is that way and there is nothing we can do about it.

Andrew: I don't know.

They let him sob for a while.

Man 1: Comrade, I don't suppose you know who we are.

Andrew: Soldiers?

Man 1: No comrade, we are comrades.

Andrew: Guerrillas? Excuse me but your uniform.

Man 1: You cannot always tell by the uniforms comrade, sometimes we wear uniforms, sometimes we wear ordinary clothes.

Andrew: Please forgive my mistake.

Man 2: Oh, comrade there is nothing to forgive, we came to pay our respects to you, we grieve for your father with you, this shelter is in our operational area, we take care of the old people in it, supply them with food, medicines, and other necessities that we liberate from the Ian Smith government. No government personnel have ever come here since we moved in.

Andrew: I cannot tell you how honoured I am, sons of the soil of Zimbabwe. Uh! (*He sighs*) Your presence here today is not a coincidence. That you should be here in the shadow of my father's death, signals the end of my journey to come over to you to join you, our freedom fighters, fighting to liberate our country. I struggled and prayed and cried to our ancestors' spirits to find me a job to give my father a pillow to rest his weary head on. After a long time, I was blessed, they heard my anguished cry, and they gave me a job, it isn't much but it's a job with dignity where I get paid, and I look after my father. A place to take my father's life away from disrespect and my sister-in-law's abuse. To hear the laughter from the depths of his heart calling my mother telling her that all was well again. But all was in vain, I never got a chance to show my father the job I got and his new home in the servants' quarters of another rich man's home.

And now he is gone, gone, away from the misery, shame, and disgrace that his son brought upon him. Yes, my father has sent you to take me with you. His spirit has called you my brothers to sit here with me. I am ready, I will go with you.

Man 1: The spirits work that way comrade; we will be glad to have you fight for Zimbabwe with us. The struggle needs comrades like you.

Andrew: I thank you.

Man 2: But for now, you must think of the burial of your father.

Andrew: I could bury him here myself; it wouldn't make any difference to my brother.

Man 1: We will help you bury him.

Andrew: You will help me?

Man 1: Of course. It is our honoured duty. Just like you, we are your father's children too. We are Africans.

Man 2: Death unites the strong, you are strong comrade.

Andrew: Thank you very much, I do thank you.

Man 1: Comrade, even though you will be burying your father here, we would like to ask you to go to Salisbury as you intended.

Andrew: To Salisbury? I don't have anything to go to Salisbury for, When I said I was ready to join you, I meant now, I want to be like you. To carry the guns of revolution like you, here and all over the land, I want to crawl into the soil of our country and blend with its blackness digging the furrows of our freedom, to honour my mother's death and the life that was usurped from my father. I want to be on the frontline. I don't want to be in Salisbury.

Man 2: Making the casket to bury your father in will take a day comrade. We have a package that must be delivered to a man in Salisbury,

Andrew: I see, what kind of package is it?

Man 1: A very important package, taking it to Salisbury would be your first big win in the struggle against Ian Smith. It is not an ordinary package that you will be taking to Salisbury. It is a bomb.

Andrew: A bomb?

Man1: Yes, a bomb

Man 2: It's not a big, big bomb. But if it detonates in close quarters, the results are horrific.

Man 1: I am sure you have heard of bombs going off in Salisbury.

Andrew: Yes, last Saturday a big postal mailbox was blown by a bomb.

Man 2: It only happens on weekends because people are off from work. Our bombing is not done during the week because innocent people are at work in the city during the week. We don't want to injure innocent people at work or passing by. But weekends, yes, these small bombs go off in different places. It sends a message of terror to Rhodesia Government, that is why they call us terrorists.

Andrew: Uhmm, I understand. So how would I carry a bomb? Isn't it dangerous?

Man 1: No, it's not.

Andrew: Really?

Man 1: Really. You will simply carry the package and deliver it to our contact in Salisbury. After you return on the next bus, we will help you bury your father and then escort you to our base camps in Mozambique where you will get your training.

Man 2: Don't be afraid, no one will know you are carrying a bomb. We have been doing this for a while now. All you have to do is carry it as I am carrying it. See there is no danger. Most important - the wires are not connected. But I must be honest with you, even though the wires are not connected It will explode if it falls on a hard surface.

Man 1: Can you, do it?

Andrew: Yes, and if I am going to Salisbury, I might as well go and tell my brother of our father's death. I am going to gouge him with the news. I want to see the look on his wife's face when I spit on him.

Man 1: The bus you are taking will arrive in Salisbury in the night, so you won't be able to deliver the package until tomorrow morning.

Andrew: Where do I take it?

Man1: You will take it to number 25 Msasa Close in National Township, do you know where that is?

Andrew: I know where Msasa Close is. Yes, I can find it.

Man 1: The person you want to give it has a scar on his forehead, on the left side. His name is Tapera, he is expecting it. You understand?

Andrew: Yes, I will give it to Tapera at 25 number Msasa Close in National.

Man 1: Thank you. In the meantime, we will make the casket for your father's burial while you are gone. Don't worry about it anymore.

Andrew: Thank you, thank you so very much, sons of the soil.

CURTAIN

HIGH CLASS NATIVES
Ballroom Dancers & Mbira Players

ACT Nine

Scene 1

Choto's House same night

When the curtain opens, funk music is playing.
There is a party in progress. The house is full of guests. White, Indian, Coloureds
and Africans. The music is loud. There is dancing in the cleared living room floor.
Some of the guests and their hosts, Sally and Rwizi, had too much to drink. They
are all dressed in formal ballroom dancing attire including Belinda, her husband
Sam and John who is mingling with the dancing and drinking guests. Arimando
is dressed in his uniform, throughout this scene he will be walking around the room
collecting the empty glasses and bottles.
As the curtain rises the dancing continues for a short while, the record ends. A
photographer is taking pictures.

The Master of Ceremony, an African man, James Goto, holding a shiny gold plated
trophy, asks for silence.
h

    Goto: Ladies and gentlemen, may I have your attention please.

(There is a measure of silence)

    Goto: The way we are going, this is going to be an all-night
    affair, so please indulge me for a moment to ask our guest of
    honour Mr. Simon McIntyre, to propose a toast and present
    the trophy to our 1977 Rhodesia Ballroom Dancing
    Champions, our host and hostess, Mr. & Mrs. Choto.

There is a general round of applause as Simon McIntyre, one of the white guests,
comes forward to propose the toast.
With the announcement, Sally and Rwizi who had been standing separately
mingling with the guests, come together joined by Belinda, Sam, and John. They
stand by the wall surrounded by two couples, one white, one Indian.

    McIntyre: Thank you, thank you very much. This is a great
    honour, ladies, and gentlemen. It gives me great pleasure to be

152

here to celebrate our 1977 Rhodesia Ballroom Dancing Association champions, Sally and Rwizi Choto. I can't help but say that it is occasions like this that typify our beautiful Rhodesian society. This occasion is an example of the friendship across the colour lines that we enjoy in Rhodesia. Our communist enemies in London and Maputo who accuse our government of oppressing the Africans do not know what they are talking about because they refuse to see the truth, this occasion is evidence of that truth.

Look at Sally and Rwizi, they are an example of African prosperity in Rhodesia. They show that every African who works hard and gets himself an education has the same opportunity as the whites, the Indians, and the Coloureds in Rhodesia. This wonderful couple is not the only one. Look around this room, it spells success, doesn't it?

Guests: Hear! Hear!

McIntyre: Before I present the trophy and toast our champions, Rwizi and Sally, I want to make a statement. I don't want to make this a political toast, but it hurts so when these Zapu and Zanu communists in Maputo and Lusaka lie and accuse white people in Rhodesia of being racists. The Rhodesia Ballroom Dancing Association has different ballroom dancing clubs under its umbrella, each race with its own club and its own residential area, but I can come here, to an African house to a party and so can Sally and Rwizi come to mine. Our ballroom dancing association is a good example of racial harmony in Rhodesia.

Guests: Hear! Hear!

While McIntyre is making his speech.
Andrew enters from the road. He is dressed poorly. The brown paper bag with his father's clothes and hat is in one hand and the other paper bag with the bomb package is in the other. He stands by the door while McIntyre is proposing the toast.

153

McIntyre: This graceful couple deserved to win over us, especially some of us who have two left feet...

(Laughter)

John notices Andrew standing at the partially open door and begins to move towards it.

McIntyre: Ladies and gentlemen it is my great pleasure to toast the Rhodesia Ballroom Dancing Association Champions for 1977, Sally and Rwizi Choto.

Glasses click as they toast their hosts.

John reaches the door and opens it.

Guests: Cheers, cheers.
For they are a jolly good couple,
For they are a jolly good couple,

John: Uncle Andrew, where have you been? There is a party going on, mom and dad won, come in.

Andrew: Hello John, call your father for me.

John: Come in, there is a party.

Andrew: After I speak to your father, go on, call him.

Guests: And so says all of us,
And so says all of us,
For they are a jolly good couple,
For they are a jolly good couple,

Andrew observes the party from the door.
John returns to the veranda leading his father by hand. (Rwizi is a little tipsy).

154

Rwizi: Oh, look who's here…hesi Mupamombe. I am so happy you went and got our father. Where is dad?

Andrew: I have bad news, mukoma.

Rwizi: What could be so bad on a party night like this? Whatever it is, I will fix it. Wait here, let me get Arimando to get you some food and something to drink. Tonight, you and dad sleep in his room. He can sleep anywhere, I don't care. Let me go get him to…

Rwizi turns to go back into the house. Andrew turns him back holding his shoulders.

Andrew: Wait, wait…I have come to tell that Baba is dead.

Rwizi: What are you talking about? Baba is dead? He can't be.

Andrew: Yes, he is dead and all that's left of his belongings is in this paper bag. I came to tell you about it and now I go back to bury him, there in Plumtree where you sent him to die.

Rwizi: Baba is dead? Dead?

Andrew: Yes. He is dead. Dead all by himself in Plumtree at the place you sent him. Now I am on my way back to bury him.

Rwizi in his drunken state starts crying.

John: Dad, why are you crying? Why is sekuru dead?

Rwizi slumps down on the edge of the veranda floor. John sits next to him. They are both sobbing. Andrew looks down at them as he remains standing clutching the two paper bags in his hand.

Out of the corner of her eye, Sally sees Andrew and rushes to the door. She is, like Rwizi, also a little tipsy from the alcohol. She pushes Andrew to the other corner of the veranda before noticing Rwizi and John sitting behind her on the floor sobbing.

Sally: What are you doing here?

Andrew: I have come to talk to my brother.

Sally: You have come to spoil my party. That's what you've come to do. You people won't leave us alone. Uh? You don't want to see us enjoy ourselves, do you?

Andrew: I didn't know you had a party.

Sally: Now you know. Go. You can talk to your brother some other time at his office.

Rwizi barely whispers a shout to Sally with John wiping away his tears.

Rwizi: Sally leave him alone.

Sally: What? Leave him alone. No. Andrew, I said go! You want to embarrass us in front of our friends. Look at the way you are dressed. You didn't even wash yourself.

Rwizi continues to sit shaking his head.

Rwizi: Sally I said, leave him alone. My father is dead.

Sally turns to Rwizi.

Sally: Is that why you are sitting on the dirty floor in your new suit? I already knew that. My friend, Mary, the matron, called to tell me. I was going to tell you in the morning after the party.

Sally turns back to Andrew:

Sally: And you, why did you have to come out here tonight in the middle of our party of the year with our ballroom dancing friends to tell him that? Couldn't you have waited until morning when our friends are gone? I was going to tell him.

Andrew: I don't have to take this from you. I am not my brother Rwizi whom you have tamed like your servant Arimando.

Rwizi springs to his feet and grabs his wife by her shoulders and turns her around.

Rwizi: Sally, you knew my father was dead and you didn't tell me? I said, leave my brother alone. My father is dead.

Sally cuts him off with her icy voice.

Sally: I am sorry. Yes, I heard you but…

Rwizi: My brother is not going anywhere.

John: Mummy leave uncle Andrew alone and daddy is crying…

Sally: Hush John…

Rwizi: No Sally, you hush.

Sally: No, I will not be quiet and let your uncouth kaffir brother come to my house and embarrass me in front of my high class friends.

As Sally insults Andrew she pushes Rwizi aside and lunges at Andrew. As Andrew staggers backwards, the bag with what is left of his father's earthly possessions is caught in Sally's pointing finger and tears scattering Majasi's hat, shirt, bangles and old shoes on the ground. Andrew staggers backwards and falls

157

on his back with both his hands clutching the brown paper bag with the bomb package on his chest against his body.

Rwizi grabs Sally to stop her from going after Andrew.

John: Mummy don't hit Uncle Andrew.

Rwizi: Sally go back into the house now! Go and be with your high-class friends. My father is dead. What a fool I have been. Go, go, now! John has seen enough disgraceful adult behavior for one night. Go before I do something I will regret. I have been such a stupid fool. I said GO back to your precious party now. I want to mourn my father in peace!

Sally: If you don't come back in there with me, what will I say to our friends, our guests…?

Rwizi: I do not care. Tell them anything. I don't care. Tell them my father is dead! Tell them the same lie you always tell them when I skip dance practices to   attend African liberation political meetings.

As Sally turns to walk back into the house.

Sally: Come John…

John: No, I don't want to be with you and your friends. I want to stay with dad and Uncle Andrew. Dad, can I stay out here with you and Uncle Andrew? You and mommy said there's no bedtime for me tonight.

Sally walks back into the house alone.

Rwizi: John, go into our bedroom and bring me my wallet and car keys. They are on mommy's dressing table.

Rwizi turns to Andrew who is still sitting on the ground cradling the paper bag with the bomb package.

Rwizi sits down on the ground next to Andrew.

Rwizi: I have no idea how I am going to go forward with my life. I have killed my father. The man who made me and sold his cattle so I could get a BA and buy this house. And I have allowed this woman to throw him out. My ancestors, where do I turn to hide my shame. My ancestors, how do I ask for forgiveness. There is nothing that my father would not do for me. He even went to his death in that forsaken Plumtree old people's home just so that I would be happy with my so-called wife. Mother, oh my mother, Mukumbudzi, please hear me. Please ask my father to forgive me. Tell my father, though I am a grown man, I am a fool, no wiser than his grandson John. I will make amends. I will go and get his body. I will take it to our village in Mhondoro and bury him next to you. I do not care about police and soldier roadblocks or Ian Smith government law. I do not care about any of that white man's bullshit. I will give my father a proper Mupamombe African traditional burial. There will be a bhira to celebrate Majasi's life. I am your child I belong with you my ancestors, this is your country, this is our country. My father's body belongs in our home. I wronged you my father in his life, I will not wrong you in death.

John returns with his father's wallet and car keys, followed by Belinda who comes out to see what is going on.

Rwizi turns to Andrew.

Rwizi: Mupamombe get up.

Belinda notices Majasi's hat on the ground.

159

Belinda: Rwizi what is going on? Why is sekuru's hat on the ground.

Rwizi *(despondent):* My father is dead.

Belinda: Sekuru dead? What? Where is he?

Rwizi: Plumtree

Belinda *(as she picks up the hat)*: Plumtree? What are you saying? Why is he in Plumtree?

Rwizi: Go ask your friend in there. Me, my brother, and my son are driving to go get his body now. We will bury him in Mhondoro next to my mother.

Belinda (with tears in her eyes): Rwizi, I am so sorry sekuru is dead, He was such a great man. I am so sorry.

Rwizi: We must go now. I do not care about Sally's highfalutin party anymore.

Belinda (crying): How could this happen?

Rwizi: Ask Sally. I have no answers.

Rwizi turns to John.

Rwizi: John, we are going to Plumtree right now. Pick up your grandfather's things and put them in that bag your uncle is holding.

Andrew: No, mukoma, we cannot put our father's things in this bag. There is a package in there from our boys in the bush. We must deliver the package here in National on our way to Plumtree to see about baba.

160

Belinda is crying, holding Majasi's hat as the lights fade to black.

(Fade Lights Out)

EPILOGUE

Scene 2

(Fade in Lights.)

When the lights come on, we are in Choto's living room. The guests have left.
Belinda still holding Majasi's hat, is standing being consoled by Sam.
Sally is sitting in a chair alone, holding the ballroom champion trophy.

Sam: Can someone tell me what's going on? Belinda why are you crying, and Sally is sitting there not saying anything. Sally, what's going on?

Sally (talking to herself): That Andrew ruined everything. (Shaking her head) Did you see how my guests just left my party? The MC just handed me this trophy when he was leaving like it was an afterthought. I didn't even get a chance to make my speech. Rwizi left. The photographer left. Our picture will not be in the newspaper tomorrow. That Andrew ruined everything. Why? Why? Why.

Sam: Belinda, what happened while I was in the bathroom? What is going on with Sally? What is she talking about?

Belinda: I do not know. Rwizi said to ask Sally why his father was in Plumtree.

Sally (talking to herself): There will be no pictures of me with my trophy in the paper, no pictures of me and my husband in the newspaper tomorrow. Why did everyone just leave when the party was going on so well?

Belinda: I told them that Rwizi's father, who I thought was sleeping in the bedroom, was dead. I told them Rwizi was not coming back to the party. That's why they left; it was not appropriate to be dancing in the house of a dead man.

Sally: But Rwizi's father is not dead in this house, he is dead in Plumtree.

Sam: Dead in Plumtree? What is he doing in Plumtree?

Sally: I found him a very nice old people's home in Plumtree where he would be with people his own age, his own kind. I suggested that Rwizi place him there because it was well recommended by my friend Matron Katatu and, with this war going on, it was the best place, I could find.

Sam: You did what? I am confused. Why would Rwizi agree to put his father in a desperate place meant for foreign Africans who have no family in this country. I do not understand that. You are Sekuru Majasi's family, why did he need to be in such a place.

Sally: He did not belong here in our house. With his African ways, he was not a good influence on my son, John. We are a European cultured family. Didn't you see all the white people, Coloureds and Indians who came to our party? I wanted to have the championship party here in our house with people who are only like us. Rwizi's father did not belong here because he spoke in Shona in the house where I am teaching our son John to speak in English only. I told Rwizi he would be better off with other old Shona speaking Africans living somewhere else that's why I found him the place in Plumtree. Now it's all ruined because he is dead over there and Rwizi left me just as I knew he would if I had told him. That's why I had not told him that his father was dead.

Belinda: What do you mean? You already knew that his father was dead? You knew it along?

Sally: Yes, my friend, Matron Katatu called and told me. He died two days ago.

165

Belinda: What?

Sally: I was going to tell him tomorrow after the party. I just wanted our guests to have a good time at the party and have our pictures with this trophy in the newspaper. But that Andrew had to come tonight and tell him, just to spoil it for me. He ruined the only chance I had to show my white friends that we are not ordinary Africans. (*Quietly sobbing*) Oh my god! No pictures in the newspaper.

Belinda: Never mind your pictures and your white so-called friends. Two days ago, you were told that your husband's father was dead. He died two days ago, and you didn't tell him? What is wrong with you? You don't see anything wrong with what you did?

Sally: What difference would it have made if I had told him then, his father was already dead? I know my husband; I know how he thinks. If I had told him his father was dead, he would have abandoned everything I have worked hard for to win the European classical music ballroom dancing championship as we did. He would have left me by myself, and I would have not won the championship trophy by myself because I dance best when I am with Rwizi. He knows how to move my body. Rwizi would have told me to get another ballroom dance partner and host this party all by myself. So, it was best to wait to tell him when I knew we would have time for funerals. Until now, we did not have time for that. It was about winning the Rhodesia Ballroom Dancing Association champion trophy and getting our pictures in the society pages of the newspapers. (She pauses) You know, I cannot believe that after all this, that newspaper photographer didn't even take a picture of me holding the trophy. He just left with everyone. It was all for nothing. (*She sobs*)

166

Belinda: You are a mad woman. Mad. Mad. Yes, I agree, if you are ruined, it is your own fault. After throwing your father-in-law out of his own son's house because you wanted to have this silly party, you added insult to injury, by not to telling his son, your husband, that his father had been dead for two days. It is unconscionable that you sent that great man to his death like that. You are a professional medical person. Sekuru Majasi was not well. You know that. He was the pillar of your family. You are a mad woman - to put away the pillar of your family just so you can have a party with these pretentious ballroom dancers and have your picture in the newspaper? Sally, you hardly know these people. See? Did any of them even express their condolences to you when they made a bee line out of your house? No. You know why? Because they do not know you and chances are they do not even care.

Sally: Bee, you are talking like my husband now. It is not fair. You are blaming me for his father's death.

Belinda: The way you have acted, you might as well have put a pillow over his face and suffocated him to death yourself. Yes, your actions contributed to his death.

Sally: No, I didn't kill him. Rwizi knows it too, I didn't kill his father. But he left here, angry with me. It is not fair. He took my son with him. I do not know what to do. Rwizi and my son are the only family I have. What is going to happen to me? He cannot blame me for the death of his father. How was I supposed to know the man was going to die in Plumtree? What am I going to do?

Sam: You better get yourself together and think about how you are going to make this right.

Sally: I do not know what to do.

Belinda: First throw away that stupid ballroom dancing trophy you are holding. Throw it in the rubbish bin where your husband will never see it again. Follow him. You had better catch up with him and tell him you are sorry before he buries his father and your marriage with it.

Sally: I have ruined everything. I don't know what to do. I don't know what to do.

Belinda: I am so upset with you and your obsession with all things European. I have a good mind to just leave you and your miserable pretend European life.

Sam: No honey. You cannot just leave. She is your friend; we will drive to Plumtree with her and go to Mhondoro and help Rwizi bury his father.

Sally: Oh, my thank you Sam. Thank you Bee.

Belinda: Alright, change your clothes. We do not have much time. Find a dhoek to cover your head and a Zambia wraparound cloth for your dress for the funeral. We will pick you up in a few hours.

Sally: But I do not need a Zambia wraparound cloth, that's for poor women. I will wear that black dress. The civilized thing is to just wear black to a funeral.

Belinda is exasperated.

Belinda: No, no the black dress you are talking about is not long enough to wear to a funeral. It is not proper attire for a woman. It would be disrespectful in our traditional African society. (*Shakes her head*) I do not know any African woman in our country who doesn't have a Zambia wraparound cloth to go to funerals with. Well, I hope you have something to cover your head, and I don't mean an English tea hat either.

Sally: I have a doek to cover my head.

Belinda: Very well then, my husband and I are driving to Sekuru Majasi's funeral to honour him. He is our friend's father and he was a great human being. And I am going there, to place his hat on his coffin because we loved him so. And, you, Sally, can do whatever you want.

Sally: I am coming with you. Thank you.

CURTAIN

END

www.ingramcontent.com/pod-product-compliance
Lightning Source LLC
Chambersburg PA
CBHW031528120626
46545CB00005B/2041